PRAISE FOR PATRICK DOBSON'S
Seldom Seen: A Journey into the Great Plains

"An important addition to the growing body of nonfiction literature from the Great Plains, *Seldom Seen* highlights the quiet, forgotten lives of America's rural center. Whether touching or discomfiting, these ordinary lives, like grace notes, make Dobson's journey into the Great Plains unexpectedly luminous."
—Susan Naramore Maher,
Western American Literature

"With open eyes and open heart, Patrick Dobson shows us the heart of the nation."
—David Shribman, executive editor of the *Pittsburgh Post-Gazette* and syndicated columnist with Universal Press

"The prairie, lovingly described by the author, becomes the fabric that holds these people together. Their stories, some as violent and powerful as a Midwestern thunderstorm, others as calm as a breeze, create a captivating narrative, and Dobson finds the common humanity that keeps people struggling against their circumstances and striving to succeed, in whatever form that may take."
—*Kirkus Reviews*

"Dobson offers visceral descriptions of his surroundings, which draw readers into his story at a sensory level. . . . Such beautifully written natural scenes will satiate those who come to this book hoping to be swept along with Dobson on his journey."
—Traci J. Macnamara, NewWest.net

"[*Seldom Seen*] is a dynamic portrait of a man in the process of arriving, step by step, at a better self."
—Nina Shevchuk-Murray,
Nebraska Life

"This intimate search for self-discovery and renewal is so well told, you'll smell the dew on the morning grass, and you'll know you've found something truly delicious. I've put in more than 100,000 miles, some on these very highways. Dobson paints a clearer portrait with words than I ever captured with cameras. Bravo!"
—Michael Murphy, coauthor of *Rare Visions and Roadside Revelations* and vice president of programming for Kansas City Public Television

"A journey worth taking."
—David Pitt, *Booklist*

"Lighting out for the territories—as Mark Twain would have put it—Patrick Dobson discovers his country, his neighbors, himself. Peter Jenkins (*A Walk across America*) meets Robert Pirsig (*Zen and the Art of Motorcycle Maintenance*). *Seldom Seen* inspires the adventurer in me—as it should all of us—to go out and do something similar."
—Eddy L. Harris, author of *Mississippi Solo: A River Quest* and *Still Life in Harlem*

CANOEING THE GREAT PLAINS

A Missouri River Summer

PATRICK DOBSON

UNIVERSITY OF NEBRASKA PRESS
Lincoln and London

Library of Congress
Cataloging-in-Publication Data

Dobson, Patrick.
Canoeing the Great Plains: a Missouri
River summer / Patrick Dobson.
pages cm
ISBN 978-0-8032-7188-3 (hardback: alkaline
paper)—ISBN 978-0-8032-7443-3 (epub)—ISBN
978-0-8032-7444-0 (mobi)—ISBN 978-0-8032-
7445-7 (pdf) 1. Missouri River—Description
and travel. 2. Great Plains—Description and
travel. 3. Dobson, Patrick—Travel—Missouri
River. 4. Dobson, Patrick—Travel—Great
Plains. 5. Canoes and canoeing—Missouri
River. 6. River life—Missouri River. 7.
Self-actualization (Psychology) I. Title.
F598.D58 2015
797.12209778—dc23
2014043936

Set in Fournier by Lindsey Auten.
Designed by N. Putens.

This book is for my brother and my friend, Joachim Frick
August 13, 1962–December 16, 2011

The genius of the United States is not best or most in its executives or legislatures, nor in its ambassadors or authors or colleges or churches or parlors, nor even in its newspapers or inventors . . . but always most in the common people.
WALT WHITMAN, Preface to the 1855 Edition of *Leaves of Grass*

I have come to look upon the Missouri as something more than a stream of muddy water. It gave me my first big boy dreams. It was my ocean. I remember well the first time I looked upon my turbulent friend, who has since become as a brother to me.
JOHN G. NEIHARDT, *The River and I*

Contents

Acknowledgments

AUTHORS USUALLY TAKE FULL CREDIT FOR THEIR WORK. But I don't lie and can't tell you I wrote this book by myself. Family, friends, and strangers—more than I can mention here—listened as I worked out my thoughts. Some of them read this manuscript and told me when the writing did not work. Others pointed out when the tale took off on silly tangents. Editors, critics, and friendly opponents encouraged me when I was sure I was worn out, cooked, done.

On the other hand, I take responsibility for anything in this book that embarrasses me as a writer. No one else plays a role in my folly.

I am not a strong man, nor do I have much talent. I know hard work, and I'd have failed in that if not for my family—Virginia, Sydney, and Nicholas. They aided me when I was discouraged, exhausted, and fed up with myself. Bridget Barry of the University of Nebraska Press listened to me in moments of despair, overexuberance, and the range of emotion in between. Without her direction this would be a far weaker and perhaps unreadable tale. Eddy L. Harris's work changed my life, and his continuing encouragement drove me forward. Everyone needs a friend like him.

I wrote the first draft of this book in the University of Missouri–Kansas City Department of History graduate office in the summer 2005. From that moment forward, Dr. Louis Potts and Dr. John Herron tolerated my creative work as I studied for a doctorate in their field. Dr. Potts prodded me to take academic and creative work seriously. Dr. Herron, my dissertation director, inspired and motivated me as a writer. Dr. Steven Dilks and Dr. Daniel Mahala encouraged me through their experience and example.

I owe debts I cannot repay to Dr. William Neaves of the Stowers

Institute for Medical Research and to Dick Furtwengler. They pointed out the strengths and flaws of the first workable drafts of this story. They labored like yeoman, considering the state the manuscript I set them.

Joachim Frick, Rev. David Dechant, and Patrick O'Kelley shaped the story you will read now. Joachim once told me, "You'll be happier when you stop worrying about what you believe everyone thinks about you. Please, shut up and write. You'll be fine. I promise." Rev. Dechant pressed me to quit hiding and to expose myself in the tale. Patrick understood the story better than I and saw connections in it that I could not. All of them are amazing thinkers and scholars, and I'd be less of a person without them.

My brothers and sisters in Kansas City Ironworkers Local Union #10 are giants who know determination, grit, and a job well done. Geniuses walk among them. I want to thank Jim Atkinson and Brian Garrett as well as Jeanne Park of San Francisco Ironworkers Local Union #377. Sometimes I kept going just because they said I could.

Greg Martin, associate professor in the Department of English at the University of New Mexico, is an author and scholar of great accomplishment. When I thought the manuscript was ready for your eyes, Greg suggested a further revision that changed the entire scope and course of the narrative. Thank goodness Bridget found him.

Finally, I thank all the people who discouraged me or reviled my work. For nearly five decades, teachers, family members, strangers, as well as some of my fellow students, writers, and poets worked doggedly to convince me I could not write. I needed "to show them," until I didn't have to prove anything to anyone anymore.

Prologue

I STEPPED OFF THE PORCH AND INTO THE GREAT PLAINS.
Big sky and flat horizons made me feel how small I really was. But
letting go terrified me, until something snapped. I fell into peaceful,
all-encompassing obscurity. The road swept me away, one step and one
more in an endless stream that led me to a riverbank far from home.

I saw my reflection in the river and felt the thrill I get standing on the
lip of a canyon or a bridge over a ravine. The magnetism of love and
dreams and yearning made me spring into that void called the Missouri,
not to die, but to live.

1 Doomed

I STEPPED OFF MY PORCH IN KANSAS CITY AND INTO THE Great Plains on May 1, 1995. It was one of those crisp, sunny midwestern mornings that erases bad memories and fills me with hope of my salvation. For the next two and half months, I trekked fourteen-hundred-plus miles through landscapes so beautiful they hurt my senses. My journey took me through the difficult terrains of being me, a hardheaded guy who, at that moment, wanted and needed to find more in life than working and dying. I thought I found that in the Great Plains. Then I wound up on the bank of the Missouri River outside Helena, Montana, and understood how much farther I needed to go.

That day, July 15, the river, swollen with spring rains and snowmelt sluicing down from the Montana Rockies, wrapped sinewy emerald currents around the bridge pillars and through the grass where it fled its banks. I had only one thought, likely the one that saved me a lifetime of disappointment: I was going home on this river. I had come too far and learned too much. I wasn't turning back.

As I walked across the prairies and among fields of wheat and corn, my conception of the Missouri was that of a child's. I was born in a city beside it, and all my life I drank and bathed in it from spigots and faucets. As a boy, I ran through it as it gushed from sprinklers in front yards. I dunked and splashed in it at the bright and blue municipal pool. It was the river of garden hoses and fire hydrants, fountains and fish tanks.

All across the plains, I feared discovering the Missouri was more powerful or terrible than I had heard or imagined. When the passing of a semi or a squawking goose woke me in the night, fear of the river kept me awake. My thoughts whirling in circles and my anxiety building, I reflected instead on blue-green oceans of wheat, lazy trills of meadowlarks, and people I'd met on the road. When I finally fell asleep, the river flowed through my dreams, a black line just out of sight on the other side of the wheat and corn.

On waking each morning, uncertainty about the road ahead froze me in my sleeping bag. Where was I going? What was I trying to prove? Who would I meet along the way? Where would I sleep that night? With great effort, I wrestled these thoughts aside and climbed out of that sleeping bag, dressed, and fired up my stove. As I waited for water to boil, I rolled up the sleeping bag, stuffed gear into my pack, and put on my shoes. I washed my face and hair in some sink in some bathroom somewhere. Then I drank my tea and put my shoes to the pavement.

The road took charge. Worry disappeared. After a mile or two, the sun and wind transformed my thoughts into daydreaming. I imagined bison herds stretching to the horizon. I bumped along in horse-drawn wagons, camped out with Indians, and pounded rail spikes with gangs of rough men. I dreamed of winning the lottery and giving all the money away.

Twenty-some miles later, I set up for the night in a park, some-one's yard, or on a couch. When I sat down, the day complete, my head hummed from heat and sun and the rhythm of walking. In those moments, I reflected on conversation earlier in the day with a stranger over a cup of coffee or on the shoulder of the road. Sometimes I watched the sun set without moving or thinking, until I nodded and slipped into my sleeping bag. For more than seventy days — an entire lifetime, it seems now — though the river flowed at the boundary of my dreams, it might have been as far away as the moon.

Once I arrived in Helena, I could no longer ignore the 2,200-mile ribbon of water back to Kansas City. I was frightened: the currents, the hardships, the lessons I still had to learn. Unable to bear such fear, I focused, instead, on more immediate things, just as I had each morn-ing walking across the plains. For the week I was in Helena, I gathered gear, arranged funds, and found a way to transport my boat, a sixteen-foot purple canoe, from a sporting-goods store in downtown Helena to the river.

Despite my best effort, I couldn't make the river go away. It flowed through my thoughts and the middle of my dreams. When I settled each night into the creaking bed in my bare-bulb hotel room and stared at the ceiling, I ached with the enormity of the journey ahead. Unable to sleep, I walked Helena's empty streets, wandered its alleys, and walked up into the hills to the west of town. Then, in the morning, I wrestled with the tasks at hand until the pieces came together and it was time to go.

As I stood on the bank at the Wolf Creek Bridge that July afternoon, the clouds that had hung behind the rocky sagebrush hills all afternoon blew into the valley. Within minutes, cold wind whipped the river into an angry, foamy field of white and dark green. Stinging nickel-sized raindrops splashed my fire into a smolder, the steam and smoke hugging the ground and spinning away. When the rain and cold so fogged my glasses that I couldn't see, I climbed into my tent and lay wet on my sleeping bag. I felt the river waiting behind the wind and rain.

Sometime later the wind died, and heavy rain turned into a steady drizzle. I piled the steaming remains of my fire with wet sticks, crossed the bridge, and walked along a river road. At some distance, I looked back at my campsite. The smoke from the fire rose in a wispy column. For the next two-plus months, I would live in that canoe and with those few pieces of gear. They seemed too small for such a hefty task. I was tempted to scuttle up the side of a brushy hill and get a better look downstream. But I didn't want to see or know the future. Would I have the courage to go all the way? What would the river reveal? Of itself? Of me?

On returning to my camp, I stoked the fire and watched the river from my picnic table. A truck that pulled a trailer of drift boats bounced down off the road and into the grassy field at the river access. After backing the trailer to the gravel boat ramp, a gray-haired woman stepped out of the truck and stood to the side. She wore a down vest and was sturdy as a stump. She barked orders at three men who loaded the boats with coolers, fly rods, and tackle boxes. A group of men in high-fashion fly-fishing outfits milled about looking anxious and out of place. They talked and laughed loudly, like walking through a graveyard at night. Their voices echoed over the river. Once the men climbed into the boats and set afloat on the still, opaque water, the woman walked over and sat down at the picnic table.

"Whatcha doing here?" she asked in a low, gravelly voice.

I had backpacked from Kansas City, I said. The river was my way home.

She peered at me with a wrinkled squint. Her lip curled and exposed small, stained teeth.

"You're doomed," she growled.

Before she came, I'd sat at the table, staring at the river, telling myself I wasn't going to fail. The perils were not that great. I was going to have fun and get home just fine. But when this stranger told me my journey would lead to failure, I despaired.

"I don't feel doomed," I said like a bullied kid who says, "Oh, yeah? Well, that's what you say." I didn't want to admit that I might die on this trip or, at some point, give up and go home to a life of wretched disappointment.

She harrumphed.

"You got no business out there," she said. "It's a flood year, boy. It's dangerous as hell."

Reminding me of my ineptitude was bad enough. "Boy" made me angry.

"You put people on it every day," I said. "It must be dangerous for them."

"Mister, I take city people down a little stretch of river for lots of money." She sniffed, lit a cigarette, and looked over my gear, which was in a pile by the fire. "You don't know what you're doing, do ya? You oughta turn around and go right back where you come from. That river's gonna eat you."

I slapped my journal down on the wet table and marched over to the bank. "Yeah, well, fuck you," I thought.

She was right. I'd spent all of an hour in my canoe paddling around a park lake in Helena. I'd canoed a lazy Missouri stream ten years before, when I was twenty-two. On that trip, I'd filched beer out of my friends' coolers and hard liquor from their packs and passed out in the bottom of a canoe before the middle of the first day. The rest of the weekend exists somewhere in a blackout. I don't know how I got home.

With that much know-how, then, I was starting down a big river. I counted on learning by degrees the skills I needed to get me home.

My heart raced, and my thoughts whirred in tight circles. My hands shook. The "I'll show those bastards" chip on my shoulder grew a few sizes. That defiance motivated nearly everything I'd ever done or tried. It still crops up whenever I'm intimidated and feel inept or resentful. That woman may be right, I thought to myself, but I'd prove her wrong. Regardless of the difficulties I faced, I'd pull my boat up on the bank at Kansas City and scream, "I showed you!"

I took a deep breath and stood there a minute more. On the opposite bank, a blue heron stood like a statue. Suddenly, it threw its head forward, and the water flashed. It came up with a fish in its beak. Jerking its head back, it pumped its neck and swallowed the fish. Then it took to the air and disappeared downstream with a primordial croak.

Oh, brother.

I felt the woman's gaze on the back of my neck. Did I have the wherewithal for the trip to Kansas City? Could I stand the isolation? Were there rapids and waterfalls? How would I deal with them? What would I do in storms? What kinds of people would I meet in the next two and a half months? What kinds of wildlife? Were there bears? Moose? What would I do if the boat capsized and I lost my gear? What if I was hurt? Who would save me?

I took a few more deep breaths and settled down. The river's aromas of fresh fish and cut grass filtered through my distress. The sun broke through the clouds. My vision cleared, and I watched ripples and currents snaking over the water.

I began to order my thoughts. The river terrified me the same way the walk across the plains once frightened me. In the months leading up to the trip, people warned me of dangers I'd encounter as a lone traveler on rural highways. Some even snarled at me as the woman at the picnic table did. They told apocryphal tales of murderers, rattlesnakes, and vicious dogs. Such fables, I'd learned, revealed more about what the storytellers feared than any danger I faced. I walked into Helena alive, unpoisoned, and whole.

Across the plains, through Yellowstone National Park, and past the Three Forks, I shivered in the rain and wind, slept through thunderstorms, and baked in summer heat. A pasty white business owner in Topeka mistook me for an indigent and chased me from his store with a revolver. A thunderstorm caught me outside North Platte, Nebraska, where I was the tallest thing in the landscape — no trees, buildings, or cows for miles. Lightning struck the ground so near I tasted electricity. The thunderclaps left me deaf and without even a ringing in my ears for over an hour. In Gering, Nebraska, a scrawny man with ill-defined but malicious intent followed me around town in his beat-up car. A woman in Lander, Wyoming, made ugly sexual advances toward me as her husband slept in the next room. Moose tromped around my campsite in the woods outside of Dubois, Wyoming. A homeless veteran held me hostage in a van full of cats in Jackson. In the Yellowstone backcountry, moose blocked my passage on narrow trails and bison grazed through my camp as I ate dinner. Two nights running, bears sniffed me up while I lay frozen with fear in my lean-to. I'd had a cold and the flu and suffered innumerable foot problems and several pairs of bad shoes; and once, a swarm of biting flies bloodied me.

None of it had turned me around and sent me home. Most of the way, in fact, the weather had been good for walking and animals had been gentle. I had met hundreds of people, many of them open, funny, or generous, or all three. A convenience store clerk in Beatrice, Nebraska, asked where I was from when I walked into her shop. Assuming I needed a place to stay, she tossed me the keys to her house. No questions. Just outside North Platte — after the lightning strikes — a spunky kid with a blue streak in his hair plucked me out of the rain. Through the ringing in my ears, I listened as he told me how much he wanted to be a musician. His future, he said, had to be better than the life he knew. A middle-aged corporate manager from Riverton, Wyoming, explained how he feared for his future, his career, and his personal relationships. When he dropped me off at a lonely lake on the Wind River Indian Reservation, he thanked me for letting him take me there. In Yellowstone a couple from

Boston gave me a ride in an RV big enough to house a family. While he drove, she padded about in fuzzy pink slippers and showed me postcards of all the wonderful places they'd visited. What came next for me, she said, was "sure to be nice."

These people had shown me that I make my own misery. When I left Kansas City, I dreaded a rain storm when it wasn't raining. I feared creatures when they weren't around. I worried where to stay. I feared homicidal maniacs, robbers, and just plain mean people. What I imagined was always worse than real rain storms, animals, crappy camping places, or people.

I also began to feel like an insignificant mote in the vast stretches of creation. Moose didn't move out of my way because I had someplace to go. Bears sniffed me over, though I needed sleep. Snakes, mosquitoes, and raccoons slithered, bit, and rattled around in my things with no spite toward me. Thunderstorms came and went as they do. My desire for comfort and safety didn't prevent skunks, feral cats, and wild dogs from taking food from my pack. With or without me, thunder rolled across the plains, pavement ticked in the heat, and meadowlarks sang as they lifted from fence posts. After a while, that was fine with me.

Over time, the dead showed me the comfort of powerlessness. In Nebraska, wagon ruts in limestone traced the people's paths a century and a half after their passing. In Guernsey, Wyoming, naked stones next to the Oregon Trail marked where families buried their loved ones. The blank rocks made me think of the thousands of white settlers, Native Americans, freed and escaped slaves, and soldiers who died somewhere on the Great Plains and left no traces of their lives. Even the tiny, overgrown roadside cemeteries where names and dates marked gravestones revealed how faceless and forgotten we become in death. The world moves on. A few decades and a few turns of fate might erase these cemeteries altogether.

Before, a person's disappearance into anonymity saddened me. But seeing these things, I imagined the people who had crossed the plains were like me. They had dreams of new lives, or at least better ones. They lived and struggled. They felt love, heartache, and joy. That was all anyone had the right to ask of them. It was all I had the right to ask of myself.

Canoeing home would be a different trip than journeying over land to the river. No one would drive up and ask if I wanted a ride or a place on the living room floor. I trusted my feet much more than a canoe on water. I'd have to camp and rough it more. I would have time alone, and I would have to fill it.

I cupped my hands and splashed the Missouri's cold water on my face. I possessed no talents or skills in which to put any faith or doubt. I had a canoe, tent, and sleeping bag. Waterproof bags contained food and a few other possessions. All my money was in my pocket. My direction depended on the river and my paddle. I couldn't cry to anyone. No city, town, or stranger would distract me from myself. There was nothing and no one to blame or give credit to for what would happen to me or for the experience I'd gain. Setting off into the unknown, I felt free for the first time in my life. This was my trip. The consequences, good and bad, would be mine.

The water dripped down my face and into the front of my shirt. I'd show this woman and everyone else, I said to myself. I'd walked among tornadoes, slumbered in the midst of beasts, and braved blinding thunderstorms. It would rain again. I'd swat mosquitoes and pluck ticks from my flesh. I might meet more bears, raccoons, and snakes. People were going to be selfish, but more often the opposite would be true. Anything I'd ever accomplished came out of hard work and persistence. I was good at those things, and that's how I'd push through to Kansas City.

I stood up and watched the river. I thought of Gordon, a proud Assiniboine whom I'd met in Helena a few hours after I arrived there. As I gathered and arranged gear for the river trip, he led me around the streets and alleys of Montana's capital. Over the course of the week, he introduced me to his friends—lawyers, artists, Indians, and indigent men and women. When he told them my plans, they congratulated me and wished me well. They never told me I'd fail. Gordon himself never doubted my ability or determination. As we searched for someone to ferry my canoe to the river, his friend Rico stepped forward and offered to help. He was an ornery giant of man who'd moved to Helena from inner-city Chicago. A gruff character whose manner was as confrontational as his mouth, Rico told me I was crazy. Then he smiled and said he believed in ordinary people who didn't do ordinary things.

Gordon and I roped my canoe to Rico's rusted, smoking Ford LTD. When we had unloaded my gear at the Wolf Creek Bridge, we stood on the bank, the three of us astonished at the size of the river. The river here, I had imagined, flowed about as big as the one I had seen at Three Forks—what we in Missouri would call a big creek. But this was a grown-up river, and it took me by surprise.

"This river's a good thing," Gordon said finally. His face broke into a smile. "It'll take you where you want to go."

"I got a feeling about you," said Rico, laying his catcher's mitt–sized hand on my shoulder. "Be afraid. You gotta. But keep going. You'll get to the other side. Yes, you will."

I rinsed my face in the river again and laughed out loud. At least I wasn't stealing money from rich dupes I cast to watery peril.

I walked back and apologized to the woman for stalking away so abruptly. "This is all new to me," I told her. "If I get 'et, too bad. I walked fourteen hundred miles to get here, and I'm going home on that river."

The woman huffed and scowled and told me, "Good luck." She snuffed out what was probably her fifteenth cigarette since she sat down and harrumphed again before walking over to her truck.

"I'll read about ya in the newspaper."

After she drove off, I sat at the fire. A trout slapped down against the water just off the bank. I smiled. The river would be here with or without her or me. I'd die or get home. That was that.

2 Drunkenness, Fear, and Determination

THE NEXT MORNING, I SAT ON THE BANK WITH A CUP OF coffee. The air was cold and smelled of wood smoke, wet grass, and sagebrush. There was not a human soul in sight. The swollen river sloshed through the willows along the bank, and the wind rattled the cottonwoods. The whole place was alive with frogs and crickets. As the sun peeked over the hills, its rays illuminated great clouds of insects above the river. Closer to the shore, a cormorant dropped from the air and skidded on the river, settling into a thousand fragments of light.

I ached to get on the river, but my motions were slow and leaden. I dawdled, as if putting off the inevitable would somehow turn fear into courage and chaos into order. All that water for 2,200 miles . . . Instead of packing the boat and heading off, I sat until long after the coffee had gotten cold. I built a fire and watched the river.

My head was full of contradictions. When I was growing up, the Missouri River was my Big Bad Wolf. At the breakfast or dinner table, my dad read newspaper headlines and gave sketchy details from articles about river disasters. The river flooded. Anglers drowned. Chemicals made riverside residents sick. "Someone jumped off the Broadway Bridge." "A couple of bodies washed up at Napoleon Bend." "Another oil spill at the Sugar Creek refinery." From these offhand comments, I came to know the river as dark and malevolent. It was like the sharp-toothed monster waiting to swallow me in the night if I left the closet door open.

As I grew older and learned more about the river, it grew even scarier. I read in books from my grade school and high school libraries that the

Missouri had been my city's dump, sewer, and garbage disposal. Since the founding of the Town of Kansas at Westport Landing in the 1850s, all manner of waste wound up in the river. Raw sewage oozed out of gutters and rudimentary sewers into the Missouri. Oxen and horses died in the streets, and entrepreneurs who contracted with the city hauled the carcasses off to the river. As the Town of Kansas grew into Kansas City, garbage haulers lined up at the city's river landing to throw refuse into the drink. Over time, stockyards expanded in the West Bottoms. Workers dumped the dung of millions of cows into the river, as well as the cattle that died in the open yards, stalls, and feeding pens. Meatpacking plants sluiced untold tons of offal into the river. People drank and washed in that water. Cholera, typhoid, and dysentery made them sick and killed them.

As the city grew, the river got better and worse. Progressive Era reformers agitated for sanitary sewers and water purification. Modern industry created new problems. Chemicals and petroleum fouled the river in ways far more intractable than dead horses and cow patties. Every town and city had its industry; every farmer, his or her livestock. Fertilizers and pesticides ran off farms upstream and joined wastewater from private dumps and municipal landfills. "By the 1950s," the Missouri Department of Conservation reported in 2006, "much of the lower river was seriously polluted. Garbage and giant grease balls floated on the surface, sludge deposits coated sections of the river bottom, and much of the river smelled."

As much as the bogeyman frightened me, it also intrigued me. Growing up in a suburban neighborhood, I saw the river when we crossed the Broadway Bridge on the way to the airport or on the way out of town and almost always at night. One night, when an accident halted traffic on the bridge, a towboat pushing a football field of barges rumbled beneath us. I stared, mesmerized, my nose against the window of the 1966 Dodge Polara station wagon. My siblings played. My dad complained. I couldn't understand how they could ignore the marvel below. The boat's electric-blue searchlight wandered over the water and the bank. Green and red running lights lined the behemoth as it pushed its way through a city reflected on the water. Its spotlight froze a passing train forever in my memory. Traffic began to move, but I wished there had been another boat and another after that.

As an ironworker, I build bridges. Hardly a day passes when I start my work and don't think of the river that night. I stand on the girders and remember how I felt and the sense of disappointment at driving away from the mechanical spectacle below. I carry rebar, tie it in place with wire, and watch bridge skeletons rise from the ground. I reflect on the behemoth moving through the city on the water. I come home in the evenings, fall asleep, and see the boat's lights flash through my dreams.

Before the Missouri River floods of 1977, my father took us to Kansas City's Riverfront Park a few times. There, I witnessed a universe of watery worlds. Trees shaded backwaters and vines hung lasciviously over the river. The river wrapped around abandoned barge docks and moorings just off the bank. Eddies whirled around rock dikes. Each time we went to the park, I stood at the top of the boat ramp, afraid to go near the water but wanting to all the same. The colossal currents made it seem as if the land beneath my feet moved while the river stood still. I'd stare at a spot in the stream until I tumbled off my feet. I imagined dead people, sunken riverboats, and bulky, steel barges under the rills and ripples of current.

I remember the 1972 Clean Water Act mostly because my father ranted about "the government," "damn red tape," and "bureaucracy." Despite my father's anger, factories, chemical plants, and oil refineries could no longer use the river to flush away their waste. Cities had to isolate landfill runoff from the river and build better sewage treatment plants. By 1995 when I was ready to set out on the river, I knew the Missouri was cleaner than at any time in my life. Still, doubt lurked in the back of my head and deep in my chest. I told myself that it wasn't dangerously polluted. I believed that the river wasn't poisonous or full of sewage. But in my gut it remained the bogeyman.

I couldn't stop thinking about the flood two years prior. In late spring 1993, more rain than anyone expected fell across the lower Missouri Basin at the same time that heavy snowmelt washed down from the Rockies. The river began to flood at Kansas City in early June and peaked on July 26. At that point, according to the U.S. Geological Survey, the river carried between thirteen and twenty times the water it did on an average spring day (530,000 cubic feet per second versus an average daily flow of 25,000–40,000 cubic feet per second). Upstream and downstream from Kansas City, the corps gave up saving some agricultural levees and dynamited others in an effort to lower the river and save the city's riverside industrial districts. Through town, the river threatened the downtown airport and the city's water and sewer systems. It filled the space between floodwalls on either bank like a washtub and then pushed over, flooding the industrial East and West Bottoms. Along the length of the river in Missouri, state and federal officials set up emergency shelters and evacuated thousands of citizens from flooded and flood-prone areas.

As the Missouri rose, so did its tributaries. The Grand River flowed nine feet deep through Pattonsburg. At Excelsior Springs, the Fishing River flooded lower floors of the famed Elms Hotel and the basement of the Hall of Waters, which celebrated the town's once-famous mineral springs. For several weeks at Farley, just a mile upstream from the Missouri, the tiny Platte River carried an amount of water equal to the Missouri River's average daily flow. The Platte ran through Farley's streets and ruined farms and flooded towns throughout the Platte and Little Platte Valleys. The Kansas River near Kansas City spread out as wide as an ocean over farms, parks, and residential areas. It flooded low points of Bonner Springs, Lawrence, and Kansas City, Kansas. Turkey Creek, which normally functioned as a kind of open sewer, scoured through the business and industrial district in my largely Hispanic Kansas City neighborhood. Mexican restaurants, family import businesses, and major employers along Southwest Boulevard closed and never returned. In the following years, the city demolished flood-damaged buildings. Even today, lots remain empty along streets where Turkey Creek flooded the worst.

For eight months, the Missouri and Mississippi Rivers spread out over thirty thousand square miles of land and wrecked $15 billion in property. Nearly all the flood damage on the Missouri occurred in the 818 miles of river from Yankton, South Dakota, to the Mississippi River—all below the six behemoth reservoirs stretching into Montana that the U.S. Army Corps of Engineers built to prevent such disaster. In the following years, Americans would spend $30 billion reinforcing levees, building flood-pumping stations, and reconstructing houses and factories in the floodplain. But there will be bigger floods, new challenges, and I can't help thinking that Americans will get tired of the river. I hope that someday they will just move up into the hills and let the river be itself.

That day, however, I was up against more than horror stories and memories of a flood. By the time the gruff woman confronted me at Wolf Creek, I had been sober five years. I was thirty-two and still a child in many ways. I started drinking when I was eleven. My blood contained alcohol from the time I was fourteen until I was twenty-seven. It's too easy to blame inner demons or pain or whatever and say the chaos and violence of my childhood made me an alcoholic. That's too simple and clean. I didn't drink because of one thing or another outside me, and I'd be lying to you if I said so. If I told you that demons made me do it, I'd deflect responsibility from myself. I experienced pain and violence. But in the end, I was my problem. I sought drunkenness like predators seek prey. When I wasn't drinking, I hungered for intoxication, dreamed of it, and planned my life around it. A big bottle of vodka relieved me of my personality. When I drank, I possessed no hopes and dreams. I avoided moral gray areas and human relationships. I liked being unconscious.

Nothing comes more easily to a drunk than the next best thing. Every grand idea that popped into my head took me a different direction. I started new endeavors with energy and ended them in whimpers. At one time or another, I aspired to be a racing bicyclist, a brewery owner, and a restaurant proprietor. I dreamed up thousands of schemes through which I might achieve quick wealth or adulation from an adoring and accepting public. I followed through on none of them. Bursts of wild enthusiasm preceded bouts of deep depression and self-loathing. Achieving goals was hard. Turning off was easy. I never wanted to stop drinking, because I never wanted to see the light of day. I passed out every night. I came to each morning and saw myself deeper in filth. I felt a little more hopeless. I had an excuse to start drinking again.

In the fall of 1985, just when life looked bleaker than ever, a friend called from a payphone in Hamburg. Traveling around Germany with a backpack seemed like a terrific cure for what ailed me. I sold or tossed everything I owned except for some undies, a coat, and a sleeping bag. Without one word of German, I met my friend two weeks after he called me. Sometime previously, I had become infatuated with wine and dreamed of owning a vineyard. (Regardless of my increasingly lofty attitude toward wine, I sucked up whatever swill I came across.) Once I arrived in Germany, I traveled the wine districts on trains, knocking on winery doors and asking for jobs in phrase book German. After two and a half months, I had been drunk plenty but only passed out twice — once in Berlin and another time under a bridge near Mannheim.

Still recovering from that last bender, I knocked on the right door and talked to the right man. Wolfgang Richter, the energetic CEO of the Bishop's Wineries in Trier, showed me immense compassion. He took me on as a paid intern, set me up with a room nearby, and introduced me to his staff. My coworkers treated me like an adult. They made me feel important. For a year, I lived on a $250 (500 DM) monthly salary. I worked in the Trier Cathedral's Mosel River vineyards in one of the most sublime landscapes I have ever known. My vineyard compatriots took me under their wings and taught me their German dialect. I fell into day-to-day life comfortably. After a few months, I began making friends and found the family life I'd never known, with people who lived near Trier. Josef and Marlies Frick became closer to me than my own parents. Their son, Joachim, was my brother and friend.

It was a magical time in many ways. I reinvented myself in a European city ten times older than my country. With some notable exceptions, I didn't drink as much as I had in the States. Physical work in the outdoors suited me, and I was happy in the vineyard. My coworkers and friends invited me to holiday dinners, birthday celebrations, and weddings. I fell in love with two beautiful women. One was a tender, funny, and kind German working girl. I still miss her. The other was an American opera singer, coincidentally from Kansas City, who was studying in Darmstadt. She was feisty and erotic; and being the kid I was, I chose the exotic, sexual American over the nice German girl. That summer, the American and I spent most of our time, when I wasn't drinking, in bed. I thought of her all the time and dreamed about her when she was away.

At the end of the summer in 1986 the opera singer returned to Kansas

City; and when my time at the winery came to a close in December, I did too. Like Thomas Wolfe's George Webber, I found, almost from the moment I stepped off the plane, that going home was impossible. Too much had happened. My view of the world had changed. Kansas City's lights didn't shine as brightly as I'd remembered. My hometown's streets had become narrow and cold. I felt lonely in my old crowd and noticed they felt uncomfortable around me. We ceased to have much in common. I shared a house with four men I didn't know or understand anymore and lived, literally, in a closet. Within a month of my return, the opera singer and I parted ways, our relationship a victim of too many expectations and too much drinking on my part. I took a job at a downtown pizza stand, because free beer was a fringe benefit and because I could make pizzas drunk or with a hangover. I took the bus to work and noticed for the first time the empty lots, vacant buildings, and dying blocks of the inner city. Home no longer belonged to me, and that made me sad and angry. I isolated myself, read books, and drank harder.

I jumped at the chance to return to Germany in September 1987 when the oenology school in Geisenheim accepted my application. I again dreamed of my own vineyard and winery. Despite my big ambitions, however, late nights and too much drinking made me a poor student. Several vintners needed extra help in the village where I lived. Since I had arrived there with very little money, I worked after school, running from one winery to the next. Late into the night I ran grape presses, cleared the fresh juice, and started fermentation. The winery owners paid me in cash and wine. I drank more than I ate. I was often sick and constantly afraid the tax authorities would catch up to me. Within a few months, I was broke and broken. Though I'd earned passing grades, I gave up school at the end of the semester. My friends in and near Trier put me up for a month, after which I came home without a dime or a clue.

I look back on those years and see that, like any drunk, I adjusted life to accommodate addiction. For years, I truly believed that if I paid rent and stayed drunk, I was a fabulous success. This illusion persisted despite wrecked cars, broken relationships, and increasingly squalid living. I chronically vandalized property in angry, drunken fits. I passed out in friends' and strangers' cars, yards, and houses. I stole from employers and begged money when I had to. Girlfriends left me because they couldn't deal with a child in a man's body. Some didn't want to watch self-destruction. Several of them, like the opera singer, just had good sense. When the end came in July 1990, I had alienated so many people that I had no reason to own a telephone. My boss fired me. I was sick, unemployable, living in squalor, and hiding out. I owned nothing.

I gained consciousness at the door of an AA hall and begged those people to save me. They told me the time had come to save myself. I quit drinking and attended meetings. Life went well for a few months. I felt better and found friends. I came to know dawn from waking up in it rather than passing out as the sun rose.

Then my girlfriend at the time called and said we had a baby on the way. Not yet understanding that building a new life takes time, I turned my ten-year on-and-off college career around, thinking good grades made up for wasted time. The University of Wyoming gave me a teaching assistantship. There, I worked hard to prove that I was somebody—to me, to "them," to everyone. I took it all so seriously that I often found myself in the middle of the night on my hands and knees, banging my head on the cold dorm room floor, trying to turn off my thoughts. I frequently contemplated suicide. Every long weekend, holiday, and break, I drove the fifteen-hundred-mile round-trip between Laramie and Kansas City to be with my newborn daughter, Sydney, and her mom. I made that trip twenty-three times in two years. Had I not taken to fly fishing and backpacking alone around the Snowy Range and Laramie Mountains, I might not have gotten a degree or lived through the experience.

Degree in hand and two-plus years sober, I returned to Kansas City and sought to become legitimate. At the time, I believed that meant becoming a decent dad and finding the magic job that would deliver me from inadequacy and insecurity. I pinned my hopes and expectations to every job application. Libraries, archives, and museums didn't need any more historians, especially broken ones. I suffered disappointment and self-loathing at every rejection. I constantly asked myself, "Who do I think I am, anyway? What made me think I was capable of any of this?"

The year after graduate school, my relationship with Sydney's mother ended. I blamed it on myself. At the hotel where I finally landed a job in the banquet department and then as the furniture repairman and refinisher, I worked harder and longer to get ahead, to do what was right, to become, as some would say, "bona fide." But the more I worked, the more miserable I became. I could no longer just turn off. I was facing life head-on and not doing a good job of it. I believed I was always going to be a failure.

Sydney kept me trying or at least going to work and not giving up. She was a great kid, and I was happy to be a sober father. I bought her clothes at thrift stores. I couldn't afford new toys or even used ones. Instead, she played with the plastic figurines and marbles that I brought home from banquet table centerpieces. We made a checkerboard and checkers from the bottom of a cardboard box. In place of television, we walked miles and miles through Midtown and downtown, went to free museums, and spent weekends camping. Two Christmases before I left for Montana, we wrapped my roommate's surveyor's tripod with aluminum foil and spent the day making ornaments with construction paper, crayons, scissors, and tape.

I sought challenge, a push out of unending routines and mind-numbing labor. In the spring of 1994 every lighting flash and thunderbolt reminded me of spring days on the Great Plains when the sky turns black and the wind smells of rain and grass and plowed ground. The idea of walking across the plains came to me one day at work during a thunderstorm. I thought of such a trip years before but never took it seriously or believed I'd ever make that journey. Suddenly, as lightning flashed and hail fell, I ached to get lost in the plains, go somewhere, challenge myself. Once I thought of it, the trip tested me like any whim or possibility I'd experienced in the past: "If I don't do this now," I thought, "I won't ever. I'll regret it and remain a nobody." As with all my travels, jobs, and obsessions, fear of doing nothing overcame the anxiety of doing something. Once conceived, the trip was certain.

Work gained purpose, and I found myself excited again. My goal was to cover rent, utilities, and child support for the time I would be gone. When I returned, I wanted to pick Syd up at her mom's, make up for lost time, and be the perfect dad. Her mother also deserved something extra each month for Syd's care. For the year leading up to my departure in spring 1995, I labored overtime, all the time. After eight or nine hours fixing the hotel's furniture and refinishing its antiques, I served food and poured drinks for conventioneers. I set tables for meetings of doctors and real estate agents. I bartended once at a morticians' conference. (They were actually very funny and tipped generously. Something about not taking it with you?) I polished millwork, vacuumed carpet, cleaned bathrooms, and washed dishes to pay for my trip and costs associated with keeping my house.

If I walked all the way to Helena — the biggest city farthest from Kansas City across the plains — I would take the Missouri River home. I had an excuse to get to know the river, feel its currents, and see its changes. I'd find out what it was between the contradictions. In the process, I'd discover who I was — or if there was even a "me" under the ambiguities and emotional extremes. Once I thought of it, I never considered *not* coming home on the river.

When I did have time and often when I didn't, I poured over maps and read books about the Great Plains. A small newspaper in Kansas City committed to publishing stories about the trip in notes-from-the-road fashion — my first writing job! I found a canoe maker in Maine who offered a prototype of a newly designed boat. All I had to do in exchange was to call him while I was underway and tell him how the boat handled on the river.

Between work and time with Syd, I hunted for information about canoeing the Missouri. I called dozens of local and regional canoe club members. Not one even knew anyone who had canoed the Missouri. Instead, they fed me all kinds of new horror stories: Whirlpools sucked down small boats and drowned their pilots. Barge waves flipped canoes and small boats. Catfish big as men snatched poor paddlers by the feet and dragged the poor souls into the depths. I heard about undertow, "rogue waves," and impenetrable wind, as well as deadly snakes, waterborne diseases, and poisonous chemicals. An otherwise friendly man told me that "Rednecks and Indians use people like you for target practice. Not a year goes by when someone doesn't die that way." One canoeist said he was a "veteran of challenging Missouri streams but not the

Missouri River. Oh, no sir." He went on to say, "You're an idiot, boy."
(There was that "boy" again.) One woman, after reciting a now-familiar
litany of river dangers, asked, "What kind of a person wants to canoe
that river, anyway?"

I wanted to tell her:

A guy who has a kid, a dead-end job, and vacant insides.
An alcoholic who drank most of his life away and wants to make it up.
Someone in desperate need of redemption.
Me.

But I didn't tell her any of that. I hung up on her and surrendered,
convinced I'd discover the river myself.

Now I had walked across the Great Plains and was setting out on a
Missouri River I claimed as my own—not the one I'd heard so much
about, not the one that lived in my dreams, but a being that flowed in
its valley and shaped the histories of people and nations for millennia.
I would know it the way an adult knows his or her parents. At some
point, fathers and mothers transform from gods and demons into flesh
and blood.

As I stood on that riverbank, I thought that, maybe, the Mighty Missouri was big enough to be murderer, toilet, and savior all at once. I'd
pack my things, pick up my paddle, and find out. The challenge would
strip away the burdens I'd pulled around my whole life. In the end, I
may not enjoy the river's company. I may not like who I was under all
the baggage. But I was far too tired of being afraid.

3   Your Friend, the River

AFTER MY FIRE HAD BURNED DOWN AND MORNING WAS giving over to the heat of the day, I took up notebook and water bottle and walked upstream. Past the bridge, the bank rose into small white sandstone bluffs. I sat down on the rock and unfolded a Montana highway map and ran my finger along the tiny blue line flowing through the state.

The week I was in Helena, I couldn't find a river map with names of bends, sites of rapids, or distances. A tourist brochure plucked from a rack in a tourist shop gave me a picture, albeit inadequate and cartoony, of the river's course but no clue as to miles or scale. A fat blue swath cut across the brochure with Helena at one end and Cascade, Montana, at the other. Names and phone numbers of river outfitters, adventure companies, and fishing guides filled the spaces above and below the ribbon. The highway map didn't help me understand the Missouri any better. According to the map, the driving distance from Wolf Creek to Cascade was fifty-five miles. I knew for sure the river was longer.

The map and the brochure constituted my first effort to know more about what was before me. Understanding my place in the world and the direction the river flowed put some logic to my endeavor. As I wrung my hands earlier that day, I faced infinite possibilities. I wanted to know, exactly, what to do next. Every day presents a million first steps. I get fearful trying to decide what direction to take. Will this be the right step? What happens if it's the wrong one? Will it lead to disaster? In these situations, I have to do something, anything. On the road to Helena, I stepped out of this mental mess and started with the smallest task. I found that packing my sleeping bag, for instance, or even boiling water for tea prevented me from getting ahead of myself. This wasn't an easy lesson to remember, and it was one I'd forgotten that day until I looked at the map.

A man crept around a corner in the bluff below. He held a fly rod in one hand and felt the rock ahead with the other. With my maps and the discoveries I was making with them, I didn't want company, so I laid down on my stomach to read my maps and watch him, too. He moved along until he found a ledge wide enough to stand on. Once he steadied himself, he cast into a deep-blue eddy and immediately pulled out a big rainbow trout. Then several more. He held each fish up and looked it over before releasing it gently back into the river. After he fished the hole out, he advanced to a jagged outcrop and cast upstream to a notch in the sandstone just below me.

"Enjoying the day up there?" he said, concentrating on his cast.

"You seem to know this business pretty well," I said. I was sure he hadn't seen me but now didn't know how long he'd been watching me.

He adjusted the suspenders on his waders and looked up, pulling his sunglasses from underneath his ball cap.

"I oughta," he said. "I've done this my whole life."

"You live around here?"

"I have fifteen hundred acres about ten miles north of here," he said. "It gets awfully lonely up there, and cows aren't much society. Trout are better."

"You live alone?"

"Run the whole shootin' match myself," he said. "Cows, hay, a little garden stuff. I had a wife once, but she left. I missed her for a little while. Now it's good enough when we talk on the phone every now and then. She comes up for a visit once or twice a year. I have a hell of a nice place. It's a good place to visit."

"Watch this," he said. "There's a couple I've been watching in that hole right there."

He pointed to a crack in the rock face where the water was still and clear. I peered down into the hole and saw only the dimple his fly made when it landed. In a flash, a trout zipped up out of the depths, snatched the fly, and dove with a splash. Except for the line snapping tight and the ripples on the water, it was almost as if the fish were never there.

His pole bent in an arc as he played the fish up to his feet. He lifted the big rainbow out of the water with a net.

"That was great," I said. "You catch mostly rainbows here?"

"When I'm fishing like this, I do," he said. "I get serious every now and then and go after browns. They're a little deeper, a little shier about rising to a fly. Whatcha doin' in these parts?"

I told him that I'd walked from Kansas City and that this was my first time on the river. He said he had canoed and kayaked long stretches of the Missouri. It made him happy.

"I don't think there's a better river in the world," he said.

He looked up at me and must have seen the doubt on my face. He lifted his sunglasses away from his eyes again.

"Whatever you've heard, and I know you've heard plenty," he said, "you haven't heard the river's your friend. It's always your friend. You only get hurt when you fight it."

I loved him.

He fished and we talked. I told him about long weekends I had spent fishing in the Snowy Range west of Laramie. He said he earned an agriculture degree at Kansas State University in Manhattan and had gone on to a graduate degree in biology at the University of Kansas in Lawrence, which is about forty miles west of Kansas City.

"It's pretty there," he said. "It's pretty flat, too. But it's nice out in the Flint Hills and on the prairie."

"Everyone there wants to come here," I said.

"Other side of the fence, you know," he said.

He fished up and around a corner and was gone. He didn't say goodbye.

I lay down on my back in the sun and closed my eyes. The air smelled of rain and dust and dry grass. The sun on my face reminded me of naps in the vineyard where I worked in Germany. I could smell Mosel slate and freshly pruned vines. The rock burned my back for a minute and then rendered off into a warm, comfortable glow. I remembered dark spring days in the vineyard when the rains came and put the cold into my fingers and the end of my nose.

Presently, a rain drop plopped into my eye and pulled me out of the dream. Dark clouds covered the sun, and the wind had become cold. I picked up my things and glanced over the side to see if I could spy one of those trout. But the water had turned black and opaque. By the time I dove into my tent, the rain had begun in earnest. I tried to read awhile, but the raindrops on the tent and the ground outside along with the smell of air washed clean acted as soporifics stronger than any potion or pill. I slept again for what felt like a long, long time.

I awoke in the early evening. The clouds had broken, and the sun warmed the air. I looked forward to getting on the river in the morning.

As I rebuilt my fire, an old Ford pickup pulled into the landing. Two men, young and strong with the look of people just freed from work, climbed out of the truck.

"Where the hell's your car?" one said as he walked toward me with his hand extended.

"I don't have one," I said, shaking that hand. "I'm canoeing."

"Damn fine boat you got," he said, looking around. He smiled. "I've never seen an invisible boat."

"Ha!" his pal laughed.

"I stashed it in the bushes," I said. "I'm not going out until tomorrow. It's been kind of a rough day."

"So go with us," he pointed to a battered aluminum johnboat in the bed of the pickup. An old bicycle lay on top of the boat. "We have plenty of room."

Steve Frankino, a lawyer, and Bruce Campbell, a schoolteacher, had just gotten off work and wanted to float the river for the evening. They were breezy, lighthearted people. Both were about thirty-five but looked younger. We pulled the boat off the truck and dropped it with its oars in the water. Bruce threw the bike back into the bed of the truck and jumped into the cab. Without a word, he started the truck, pulled up from the landing, and headed out toward the road.

Steve had dark hair and eyes. His shorts were frayed and his open flotation vest flopped back under his arms. We sat at my picnic table — it was beginning to feel like mine, anyway. He lit a cigarette.

"My wife hates it when I smoke," he said. He breathed deeply. As a former smoker, I could almost feel the nicotine produce the easy calm

I used to get from cigarettes. I thought his eyes were going to roll back in his head. Then, I thought mine would.

"Bruce's takin' the truck down to Craig," he said after a minute. "He'll ride back on the bicycle. It's only about five miles. We'll stick the bike in the jungle back there with your canoe and blast off.

"We do this about twice a month in the summer. In the fall, we try to sneak out on some other streams we know. It's a good break, and the river . . . well . . . it's a pretty good place to get lost."

I was glad to hear it. I also welcomed a taste of the river with some-one else before I took off on my own. Five miles! He made it sound so easy and safe. We pushed the boat into the river and took turns row-ing from the boat ramp upstream and down in the calm water next to the bank. It felt good to be on the water, even in this small way. At the end of every circuit into the river and back, we picked up the boat and dumped out the water.

We walked over to the bushes where I'd stashed my canoe. Bruce looked the boat over and approved of it.

"Jesus, you're going to have a great time," he said. He had a look in his eye that said he was imagining a trip of his own.

"Yeah, I hope so," I said. "In fact, it's good to hear that. Yesterday a stranger told me the river'd kill me."

"What does he know?" he said.

"She. What does she know?"

"Exactly."

Bruce rode up, threw the bike on his shoulder, and took it back into the long grass and brush where my boat was hidden.

"Fine boat," he said, coming out of the grass. "That your boat? It's a fine boat. Ours isn't so hot. Here, take this."

He fished a kid's orange sand bucket out of a rucksack and gave it to me. He handed a plastic cottage cheese container to Steve. For himself, he fished out a two-liter pop bottle with the top cut off.

"For bailing," he said.

We stepped into the boat and shoved off. Steve and Bruce took turns at the oars. We went only as fast as the river took us and rowed to keep the boat near the banks. We oared into side streams and around small islands. The land rolled by as if we were sitting still. I took it all in—the smells, sights, and sounds. The river was big but not as frightening or as dangerous as it looked from the bank or as I had imagined before. They didn't know it, but they showed me the river could be fun, take worries away, and allow people to be no more or less than who they were. Maybe, I thought, the river didn't strip anything from you but relieved you of the pressures of being something or somebody.

Bruce and Steve were comfortable and untroubled, happy to feel the river move them. We smoked cigars that tasted like chocolate and smelled clean and sweet. They drank beer and sipped whiskey from a bottle, which gave them lighter moods than they came with. They talked about themselves and their families with the kind of honesty that people with confidence and humility have. They asked about my journey, and my tales amazed them. The longer we talked, the more I noticed how they didn't just escape on the river but treated it as an ordinary part of their lives. The river no more frightened them than a walk in the backyard.

For three hours, we bailed, laughed at each other's jokes, and bailed some more. Once in a while, we dipped an oar in the water. We told stories. Theirs were of friends, wives, and schoolchildren. I told them about the places I'd seen and the people I'd met. I fished a little around rafts of river weed and along rocks and riffles but caught nothing. They splayed themselves out in the boat as they would on couches in the living room. As the evening lengthened, sunset ignited the river yellow and red. I felt lighter than I had since I arrived in Helena. I began to understand my journey as a process rather than as a trip through physical space and time. When we reached Craig, night had fallen. Stars danced on the river.

We packed the boat into the truck at the boat ramp and rinsed hands and feet at the bank. They thanked me for coming along. In all the years they floated the river, they said, no one else had joined them. I was glad I did them good. They had done much for me. They drove back to my camp at Wolf Creek, talking about what their wives might say and how they might use me as an excuse for staying out too long.

After they drove away, I sat on the picnic bench and stared up at the stars. Gordon, my friend from Helena, had made me a leather pouch for the small "lucky rocks" people offered me as I made my way to Montana.

I had kept them loose in my pocket. They provided a sense of comfort, a way of knowing I was not alone even if I felt so. Gordon told me the stones were "prayers" people sent with me on my journey. A day or so after Gordon gave me his gift, the pouch's leather thong had become comfortable around my neck.

I rolled the thin leather strip in my fingers. I felt at ease for the first time in a week.

4 Life Preserver

THE SUN DROVE ME FROM MY TENT WAY TOO EARLY, AS IT always does. In bare feet, I stumbled down to the river, squinting against the sunlight that flashed off its surface. I stepped in the water and an icy bolt shot up into my neck. I gasped and expelled the last of my waking sleepiness. The air was brisk and fresh, the sky clear. The wind swished down through the pines and the brushy hills. It was a good day to canoe.

I laid everything out on the bank and wrung my hands over how to get started. My mouth was dry, and my ears rung. Electricity buzzed through my chest, and my limbs felt shaky. I thought of the woman who growled at me two days before. "That river's gonna eat you," I repeated to myself. I wanted to go back to sleep. But the fly-fishing stranger assured me the river was my friend. The evening before, my lighthearted companions showed me that I should wear the river like my favorite sweater.

I decided that what mattered most was the next task, not what I might face on the Missouri in some distant future. I packed and focused on small details and heavy lifting. I worked fast and didn't think too hard. My experience as a backpacker and my intuition took over. I filled my dry bags with gear, tied the bags into the canoe, and looked after small details. I checked the ground around me, picked up my paddle, and grabbed the boat by the gunwales (the rubber edges that ran the length of the canoe). I pushed it free of the bank and stepped in. For a moment, the boat and I hung weightless between land and water. The earth and time stopped. I was not here and not there. All the agonizing of the previous days faded into distant memory. The feeling lasted only an instant. The current grabbed hold of the bow, and the world came into focus. The first breeze that I noticed smelled of crushed herbs, cold water, and trout. The boat floated sure and steady, solid. I had only a piece of wood to move me forward. The canoe was pure, a conduit that connected me to the river.

Life jacket on and cinched tight, I pushed my paddle into the water and felt the river in my hands. I possessed only the scantest idea of how this canoe thing went. While I was in Helena, the sporting-goods owner who took delivery of my canoe had recommended me to a blond giant named Reg. Helena canoers and kayakers, the store owner said, respected Reg for his whitewater skills. When I called him, he sounded irritated. Since his pal at the store told me to call, however, he said he'd meet me and see what he could do.

On the day of the lesson, Reg and I tied my purple canoe on his SUV and took it to a small Helena city park lake. Reg was shaped like an hourglass and conducted himself with that air of superiority reserved for perfect physical specimens. After we set the boat down on the sandy shore of the lake, he took up a paddle and demonstrated different paddling strokes. The slim blade looked small and toylike in his hands. He instructed me with special care in the J stroke, which he said I'd find essential. For the next hour, he yelled at me from the beach as I zigzagged over the tiny lake. He waved me in occasionally and reinstructed me. He said he didn't understand why I couldn't learn the simple J stroke that would allow me to control the canoe from one side of the boat. I apologized and put my head down, determined to please him, and went back to J stroking unsteadily around the lake. He told me to "pry," and I tipped the boat over. He told me to "pitch" or "sweep" the paddle in a wide arc that turned the boat sharply. I followed his direction and promptly pitched the canoe over again. The one thing that seemed to work, kind of, was what Reg called the "North American touring technique." For all I could see, this stroke involved just pulling the paddle straight back on one side of the boat, then the other. I understood that. It demanded no skills I didn't have. Even so, I didn't do much better touring North America on that lake than when I pitched, pried, and J stroked.

Since just about anyone knew more about canoeing than I did, I took him seriously. His basic instructions went like this:

If the boat tips over, stay with it. It will float and act as a life preserver. If you hold onto it, you can swim it to shore.

Tie all the gear down low in the boat. If the boat capsizes—which, with you, is likely—necessities will remain in the boat and won't tangle on anything in the water.

Wear a life preserver. You're gonna need it.

Stay away from sweepers, fallen trees through which the river flows as through a sieve. You get caught in a sweeper, that's bad. I don't even wanna talk about it.

Be aware of changes in the sounds the river makes. These indicate underwater hazards that might tip a craft or put a hole in it.

Don't go over a diversion dam. You can get caught for days just rolling around in the water below the dam. That's bad. I don't even wanna talk about it.

"Follow these simple rules," he said, "and you're going to get somewhere, even if you get there wet."

When this humiliation ended, I handed him a twenty for his time.

"You don't need to pay," he said, holding his hands up. "Usually I charge, but I consider this saving your life."

My disgrace complete, I tried to walk away with some dignity. I asked him if he had ever canoed the Missouri. I don't know why I didn't ask before.

"No," he said. "It's big, I know." He ran his hand through his sun-bleached hair and looked exasperated. "And I know plenty of people who tried pieces of it. I wouldn't do any of it, though. Too dangerous."

"Shit," I thought.

A week later, I put my "craft" on a river that was "too dangerous" for that giant blond hourglass of a canoeing expert. And I was having a great time. I J stroked idiotically from bank to bank. There was room. The river widened from about a hundred yards at the Wolf Creek Bridge to four and five hundred feet. Reg had done everything in his power to dissuade me from touring North America with my paddle, and I figured I'd catch on to the "J," as he called it, without his critical eye and oppressive snootiness. But the skill didn't come, and I gave up it up. For now,

I'd become expert at the North American touring technique. I liked the name. It was true to what I was doing. It was easier, intuitive, and probably the way people paddled boats for thousands of years before anyone called it a North American anything. It demanded no coordination from a brute with little physical finesse. Paddling this way, I sunk my back and arm strength, as well as my anxiety and doubt, into the river.

I had entered the river's world. The Missouri didn't buck or shoo me off but guided my boat and me with a steady and firm hand. Its currents expressed its power and reach. It flowed translucent and clean, almost as if it glowed from beneath. Like a person, its moods changed. It showed its faces when breezes broke its surface or water welled up in mushroom-like boils off its bed. When it eased around a curve or bunched up in a narrow, I felt how it adjusted in the way it moved the boat or felt in the paddle. The river still frightened me, but I was willing to go along with it and discover its personality in the way it expressed itself. I understood what the fly-angler meant when he said it would be my friend if I didn't fight it. Maybe, I thought, life would be my friend if I didn't wrest control of it and direct it my way.

The Missouri was the sinew of its valley. Everything defined itself in relation to the river. Willows and cottonwoods lined the river in a snaky green line through the otherwise dry sagebrush hills. On the outside of bends, the shore tumbled into the water down steep, rocky inclines or vertical dirt banks. There, colonies of bank swallows burrowed holes for their nests into the bare silt. Green mats of water weeds lined the banks on the inside of bends, where the land came down in a slight, long slope. Reg had told me to stay on my knees while paddling, and I did. I could feel how cold the water was through the bottom of the boat.

Bruce, Steve, and I took all evening to drift the five miles to Craig the day before. Now, those same miles flew by in less than an hour. There, at a park full of camping trailers, RVs, and sprawling family-sized tents, I stopped and filled my five-gallon water container. Soaked with rain the day previous, the campground looked like a herd of horses had stampeded through it. The kids ran and played in the muck, muddy to their ears. Parents looked resigned to the slop. People sitting in chaise lounges under RV awnings turned their heads as I pulled the canoe up to the boat ramp. It felt as if everyone had their eyes on me from the time I got out until I lugged the heavy plastic water bag back to my boat. With a smile, I sloshed through the mud and wanted to tell everyone how well I learned my new craft.

Pushing the boat into the water, I felt that eerie gap between the water and land again. The canoe slipped through eddies in the calm water and soon into the current. After Craig, the river sped up — its surface rocked with bulges and waves. But the boat held steady. My paddling skills propelled the boat mostly sideways. After a while, I gave up trying to do anything in particular with my paddle, and my boat soon headed bow-first into my future.

Feeling more comfortable by the mile, I soon got off my knees and sat on the canoe's cane seat. Boulder-strewn banks passed as if the earth rotated and the river stood still. Grasslands that blanketed the floodplain soon broke into rocky cliffs. Wildflowers studded the narrow banks and crags in the bluffs. Breaks in the walls opened into wide valleys from which hills rose like pine-crested waves. The sound of water hurrying through the branches of fallen pines or cottonwoods swished across the river.

A soft, almost imperceptible fizzing sounded through the bottom of the boat, as if my canoe floated in soda water. Puzzled, I put my ear to the gunwale and listened. A closer look at the water revealed nothing. I took a glass jar out of my gear and held it down in the river without letting it fill. Through the bottom of the jar, I could see millions of whitish flecks swirling by. Current shooting around bends and over boulders on the river bottom kicked up sand off the riverbed. I imagined billowing clouds beneath me, the plumes producing this pleasant if eerie sound.

Trout splashed where the current slowed and around beds of weeds near the banks. Unsteadily, I paddled into one of these calms and rigged my fly rod and cast. Trout bit but nothing serious came of it. Time passed without effort and ceased to have meaning.

The river narrowed as it entered a series of steep rocky hills. I had been traveling near, next to, or under I-15 all day, and it comforted me to know society was close if something went wrong. Coming around a bend, I passed under another I-15 bridge, the fifth since I left Wolf

Creek. I felt like an expert as I maneuvered the boat wide of the pillars. I screamed and yawped. My voice boomed under the bridge and launched clouds of cliff swallows from their roosts in the girders.

The water grew rougher as the river passed the confluence of a creek. Ahead, the river tumbled down in a series of standing waves, each lower than the next. All the fear I'd talked myself out of returned in a wash of panic. This wasn't foamy whitewater on a television show. The river rolled like a lake flowing down steep steps, each big enough to crush my little boat. A narrow channel broke from the main river and ran behind an island on the outside of the bend. I made for that chute, thinking I'd get out of the boat and walk it down this passage to the calm river below. I paddled toward the chute and crashed the boat into the bank above it. Stumbling out of the canoe, I guided it down the channel, believing I was a genius. The foot-deep water took a quick turn, however; and I was soon waist- and then chest-deep in the river. I panted from the cold. Panic gurgled in my throat. If this was "swimming the boat," I wanted no more of it. The water raced down an incline much steeper than the rapids in the main channel. The current was beyond my strength. The bank rose into a lichen-covered bluff. I couldn't stop or pull the boat ashore.

The current swept one foot and then the other from beneath me. I somehow flopped into the boat as a tangle of willows wrapped around and tore at my feet and legs. A shoe started coming loose. I wanted desperately to quit fighting and let the river be my friend. But this wasn't an easy relationship.

With nothing to hold it back, the canoe shot down rapids toward rocks where the water sprayed bright and white in the sun. I paddled hard, thinking Reg might find this sort of thing exciting. I pulled with my shoulders and upper body to keep the boat in the channel and off the rocks and the bluff. The water fell faster. The canoe reared up over foamy waves and plummeted into bowl-like troughs where the bow splashed under only to whoosh up again at the next wave. The river forced the boat up on its side, throwing me off balance and nearly into the water. As I pulled myself up, the canoe jerked back the other direction. My head bounced off the cross brace in front of me. Water crashed over the bow.

The boat rocketed up again toward the sky and then exploded through the tumult into the calm river below the rapids.

The sudden hush after the roar in the cataract made my ears ring. My head spun. My throat felt as if I had been playing around with wood rasps in there. Beaching on the opposite bank, where the water slowed and was calm, I sat in the boat catching my breath. A middle-aged man in waders and a fly-fishing vest walked up.

"I heard you in there," he said. "You got quite a mouth on ya. Musta been a ride."

"I didn't know I said anything," I said.

"Well, you didn't *say* anything," he said, laughing. "You screamed and yelled a lot."

Maybe the screaming had made my ears ring and throat burn. "I was scared," I said.

"I judged from your English," he said. "You fall over in there? Your stuff's pretty wet."

"No," I said. I looked down. My feet were in about five inches of water in the bottom of the boat.

"Well, son, you're bleeding right here," he pointed to his forehead.

A knot grew on my forehead where I had banged it against the canoe cross brace, which I soon discovered was called a thwart. I bent over at the waist and blotted it a few times with a towel I'd tied to the thwart for no good reason at all. My head thumped and throbbed.

"Join me for a couple of casts when you get your act together?" the man said. He nodded toward the front of my boat. Despite the rough ride, my fly rod was still lying undisturbed across my gear.

"Yeah, uh, you bet," I said, taking off my life vest. Convinced the river was going to kill me, I'd forgotten I had it on.

I stepped out. The land felt like it flowed beneath me as the river had. I had to sit down on the bank for a minute to get my legs.

Thankfully, the angler didn't use much more satire. He sensed a dented ego and didn't compound the shame with idle conversation about how I'd showed my ass.

When my heart slowed and I caught my breath, I fetched a cheap cigar from my things and considered what kind of fishing I'd find. I rigged my rod and chose a fly out of my little plastic tackle box. We compared fishing gear and talked about trout awhile, and then about ourselves. He taught history at a college in Great Falls. He came to the river to take a break from books and writing.

"It's a great place, the river," he said. "Nothing better to get my head right." I rubbed my forehead, and he laughed again. "Yours, too, it looks like."

I had to laugh.

"I've been down this stretch in a canoe before," he said. "It's quite a deal. But I would never take that chute you came out of. It's a doozy."

"I guess I accomplished something then," I said.

"More than you know," he said. "The big rapid's enough for me."

"Me, too," I said.

We stood on a grassy bank next to a meadow. I lit my cigar and started working the bank downstream. The day had grown hot. A breeze came off the hills behind and drew tiny waves across the water. Looking upstream, I realized the rapid hadn't posed great danger; the river ran there a little fast. The side chute presented a greater threat, especially as I fumbled along, guiding the boat by hand. When I sat in the boat, the water took me where it wanted, and truth be told, it flowed around rocks not into them. Regardless of my efforts to get myself hurt, I, too, had flowed with the river and around the rocks. I took a couple of deeply satisfying puffs on the cigar and smiled at my own folly.

Trade in trout wasn't furious, and the prof and I chatted for a long while.

He told me I'd arrive in Great Falls in two days. The town stood at the first of five falls over which the river descended six hundred feet in ten miles. The falls themselves stood between seven and eighty-seven feet high. Lewis and Clark, arriving at the last of the falls from downstream in June 1805, portaged their pirogues, canoes, food, and gear eighteen miles overland and continued upstream toward the Rockies. The men worked for a month walking over cacti and rocks and through aggressive wildlife. About a century later, a power company had built hydroelectric dams atop each of the falls. The dams finished the frosty plumes and dampened the terrible sound that Lewis and Clark reported seeing and hearing for many miles before they reached the falls.

I, too, would have to portage around the falls. The task had gnawed at me since I'd arrived in Helena. I thought if the problem didn't solve itself, I'd figure it out along the way. I didn't know for sure if the power company that owned the dams would take a person around them. I had no clue whom to call or what it cost, either.

"How do you get around the Great Falls?" I asked my angler friend.

"Riverside Park runs along the right side of the river there in town," the man said as he cast, carefully and easily pulling the line back over his head and casting again. "Camp just about anywhere on that waterfront. Just tell the cops what you're doing if they bother you. But get out of the water before you come to the first bridge. The river dumps down a break in the rock there and runs quickly to the first dam.

"I'd walk down to the powerhouse past the public boat dock and ask them to take you downstream. They have a truck there, and they'll find a man to pick you up at their boat ramp and take you down past the last dam."

"How much does it cost?"

"Nothing," he said. "I don't know that they have to move river travelers downstream. But they do. It's good PR for them to be decent citizens about it."

"Will there be someone there in the evening? I might be getting into the town in the afternoon or later."

"It'd be best to camp at the park," he said. "Someone will be at the powerhouse in the morning. They'll tell you how to get your boat down to their ramp safely."

He cast again and laughed a little. "They'll drop you after the last dam. Below the dam, the river goes over the Morony Rapids. They're pretty steep, with drops of six foot or more. People die there every year, almost. But you can't get on the river any farther down. The banks are too steep, almost a canyon. If you stay to the right side, you'll be relatively safe."

"Dammit." I didn't like the sound of "relatively."

"Don't worry," he said. "You'll be fine. If an old fart like me can do it, you can too."

The silence peculiar to anglers sharing their company descended on us. I sunk my energy into casting, trying to hit calm spots along the bank and put what was ahead out of my mind. After a long time without speaking, the history professor and I wandered our own ways. Soon, it was time for me to move on. I bailed out the canoe and shoved off.

The afternoon passed without incident. After my ordeal at the rapids, that was just fine with me. Everything about the river was all so new that every bend opened a fresh revelation or stunning vista. Everything played out right in front of me — nothing happened or mattered outside that moment.

I noticed how landowners marked their properties along the banks. I'd learned in Helena that in Montana a traveler could camp where they wanted on the riverbank below the "mean high-water mark." I wouldn't know from Adam what that meant. I supposed the state of Montana or the federal government measured and kept track of such things. If they didn't, property owners did. A few used purple and orange paint slashes on trees and fences to indicate where they believed trespassing on their land began. Plywood signs made clear that some of them didn't much like visitors. In Day-Glo spray paint and broad brushstrokes, the signs said, "Do not go past this line or else!!!" "Stay off," "If I see you . . . you gone too far." The outline of a big revolver on one sign left nothing else to say.

Since heavy snow had fallen in the Rockies that winter and spring rains were above average, the river ran nearly as high as it ever did. The signs and marked fence posts often stood at the river's edge, and the river inundated more than a few. I ran little chance of anyone noticing me camped out on their riverbank. Still, I squirmed at the thought of men with guns rousting me out and forcing me onto the river in the middle of the night.

A small boat landing and fishing access spread beneath a road bridge opposite the town of Cascade. I'd gone about twenty-five miles and decided my day had ended. After untying and unpacking food and gear, I built a small fire from driftwood I pulled off the bridge pillars and cooked dinner. Tired but not sore, I sat back at my fire and watched the sun set behind a mesa that rose above the tiny town. The colors in the sky reminded me of Claude Monet paintings.

The chill of evening soon settled in. My first day behind me, I felt good about my commitment to the journey. The river presented peril the way any large and moving thing does. Despite the rapids, I set myself in more danger than the river did. It wasn't going to eat me—as the woman upstream had said—at least it didn't that day.

Cascade's lights reflected off the water. Looking across the Missouri toward the little town, I claimed the river as I might claim a friend. It had its own personality and moods, and I accepted them. Canoeing demanded more than pointing the bow downstream. At the same time, the river had directed the boat more than I had. I didn't trust the river, not yet. I'd keep wearing my life vest.

Nobody drove across the bridge. A dog barked and made the silence louder. I could have been hundreds of miles from anywhere or anyone. The river muscled by in its big-shouldered way. The stars shined so brightly they hardly twinkled. I watched satellites float through the great blanket of the Milky Way. As my campfire died, my head drooped and bobbed. My sleeping bag never felt more comfortable. Coyotes bayed and yelped nearby. I soon fell asleep, and their cries echoed down the dark river and into my dreams.

5 Carless

A TRUCK BOUNCED ME OUT OF BED EARLY. RUMBLING ACROSS the bridge, it sounded like a train. I poked my head out of the tent and looked down toward the river. My stuff sprawled over the ground between the shore and me. I groaned.

On backpacking trips and camping expeditions, I wake to campsites that look and feel like they belong to someone else. The unfamiliar scatterings of gear reflect the confusion of physical exhaustion. I give up the last minutes of the day with reluctance, especially when I'm camping. Then I plod off to bed, not thinking too hard about what I leave in my wake—a flashlight here, a book there, my pack open to the elements and the animals. I fall into bed, pull off my boots or shoes, and throw them out to fill with rain.

On the way to Helena, I disciplined myself some. After all, I slept in public—in parks, on people's sofas, in strangers' yards. Communities and people provided me a sense of comfort and safety. I mustered tidiness in return. Before going to bed, I stacked my gear neatly. I hung my hand-washed undies in discreet places. I turned my shoes upside down, just in case.

But on the river, I lost all self-restraint. My campsite resembled a bomb-blast site. I didn't have much. But what I didn't have in gear I made up for in slovenly neglect.

That morning at Cascade, I must have slept hard, because the sun was full up. Time didn't matter much, but I still felt the need to move on, to get some distance before the weather changed or river slowed. My Montana state highway map showed another small road crossing the river at Ulm, which I estimated was twenty-five miles downriver. That, I thought, was a decent enough bit to travel for a day. Plus, bridge pillars meant burnable driftwood. And there are few things I like more than playing with fire.

After a cup of tea, I started picking around the edges of my mess. By the time I worked my way to the center, I'd packed all my things into two waterproof bags. In one, I stored food, most of which I bought in bulk from a health food store in Helena. This is a partial list of what I kept in the bag, packed from bottom to top in roughly this order:

Several pounds of couscous—simple to cook and easy to spice.

Coffee and tea.

Sugar for coffee and tea.

Several pounds of granola.

Dried rice and noodle dinners of the kind that I had often used on the walking trip. Add to boiling water and bing! Food.

Powdered soy milk that I thought I'd sprinkle on the granola and then add water for a morning meal. It tasted awful at first but grew on me.

Dried onions, garlic powder, salt, pepper, cayenne, and a little bottle of mustard, because yellow mustard tastes good on almost everything.

Dried apples, apricots, and cherries. I also had dried blueberries—pounds of them. If I got stranded on the bank with a broken leg, I could live for weeks on blueberries alone.

A giant jar of peanut butter, just because I'm an American and I love it. I ate it out of the jar with a spoon as I paddled.

A five-pound roll of summer sausage, which I bought lest I be too vegetarian.

My backpacker's mess kit and compact utensil set. I packed this on top—spoon for peanut butter, knife for sausage.

The glass jar I'd used to look into the river the day before. I can't tell you why I packed it, but it turned out to be a good idea.

All of this I stowed in produce-aisle baggies in case the dry bag turned out to be wet. Since I felt more secure with food nearby, I tied the dry bag to the thwart closest to my seat.

The other dry bag was sturdier. Constructed of rubberized canvas, it had shoulder straps, so I could carry it like a backpack. Heavy, warm clothes went on the bottom with extra socks, boots, and undies. Since I would only use the tent in rain or when it was really buggy, that went in next, then the sleeping bag, a couple of books, and a sophisticated first-aid kit. On top of them, I stacked some socks, a shirt, shorts, and a sweater so I wouldn't have to unpack the whole wad if I got wet or cold.

I roped the bags into the canoe by zigzagging a nylon rope between the thwarts. I laid my fly rod on top of everything for moments when I could make a few casts.

Lastly, I tied a zippered nylon bag about the size of a bread loaf to the thwart just in front of me. In this, I kept absolute necessities — pocket knife; compass; fire starter; small bottles of soap, lotion, and sunscreen; a simpler first-aid kit; toothbrush and floss; pens and notebook; a small sharpening stone; and the book I was reading. In this bag, I also stowed a plastic bag with a package of cigars and a lighter, for slow moments when a cheap smoke would hit the spot. Next to that I knotted the terry cloth towel. As with the glass jar, I just thought it might be useful. That bump on the head the day before demonstrated it was a good guess.

I took up the paddle and shoved off. That gap between land and water took me by surprise. This was, perhaps, where the river revealed its divinity. I go on river trips sometimes today just to feel it. But I can't force it. I can't launch my canoe and enter that special place on purpose. I can't be conscious of it. I've tried. That weightless release from the earth only happens when I jump into the boat without remembering it ever happened before.

I soon felt expert at this canoeing thing again. More able to control the direction of the boat, I learned the river's behavior. It changed from minute to minute, always carrying me forward. In straightaways, it flowed with nimble confidence, loping like a deer. Around curves, it twisted up like a rope. Currents wrestled and the boat rocked, sometimes gently, other times strongly. I paddled just to keep the boat in the center of the stream. The few rapids resembled the first day's terrors but little. The canoe bobbed through them like a car on a kiddie roller coaster.

By midafternoon I gained enough confidence to lean back against the stern with my butt on the floor and my calves rested up on the seat. With an ear cocked for changes in the sound of the water, I took up one of my favorite books, Bruce Chatwin's *In Patagonia*. His trip to the southern tip of South America began with his childhood fascination with a piece of prehistoric mylodon skin. His grandmother's cousin, a sailor named Charley Milward, had sent the piece of giant ground sloth hide to her in England. In his twenties Chatwin found himself dissatisfied with his job and career and set off to find the place where Charley Milward dug up that skin. That furry bit of pelt led him on a journey of self-awareness.

I wasn't looking for the burial place of a prehistoric sloth, I thought. I expected no great discoveries. Or maybe I did. I had set off to find my own Missouri and, I hoped, myself. Chatwin started his journey with more confidence, direction, and self-knowledge than I did. He knew the skin gave him an excuse for travel, which some of us are just made for. He understood that distractions in travel make the trip. At the time, I was so unlike Chatwin. I look back on my river journey and see myself as an idealistic, ill-prepared boob. I had no confidence in myself. I knew my destinations but had no clue how to get to them. A newly sober person, I knew myself not at all. But the security of ignorance works miracles. At the time, I didn't understand what I wanted. But I think it wouldn't have made one penny of difference to me. I hated my life and sought relief. I had jumped and was on my way, regardless of what came next.

At first I read with difficulty. No matter where Chatwin led me in Argentina or Chile, I popped back into the seat at every new splash and gurgle. Grabbing the paddle, I steeled myself for whatever danger made the sound. But I soon discovered that small sticks stuck in the silt near the banks ruffled the water a little. Fish flopped in backwaters. Cormorants and pelicans settled in on the river. I laughed at myself. Soon a gush or ripple caused me only to look up from my book to make sure the canoe was still in midstream. After a while I napped.

Between reading and dozing, I took in the landscape as though I had never seen woods and hills before. Every branch and rock stood out in great detail. Flowing along the front of the glaciers of the last ice age, the Missouri sawed through plates of earth rising up in its way. Bluffs of red and brown bumbled down into broad grassy hillsides studded here and there with bony pinnacles and spires. Sheets of dark stone cut through the bluffs and towered over the river like book spines. Small, gnarled pines scrabbled out a living in the crevices. Trees closer to the river grew stately and tall. Swallows popped in and out of their nests in the cut bank that sometimes rose fifteen or more feet from the water. Cows stood above me on those banks, their heads moving in unison with me as I floated by.

After a while I yawped and looked around self-consciously. Then I screamed and slapped the canoe paddle on the water with loud whacks. Gaining self-assurance, I threw deep, throaty screams up through the herds of cattle and into the hills. My voice and the smack of the paddle scared up clouds of bank swallows. Blue herons squawked as they lifted from pieces of driftwood, and pelicans turned their heads to see what the commotion was all about.

I took to yelling the only thing that came to mind, a punch line of one of Gordon's bad jokes. My voice boomed between the surface of the water and the cut bank, off the hills, and back down over the river. I shouted one word at a time and listened for the echo: PASS pass THE the TEA tea BAG bag. I changed the inflection and pronunciation of the words. I tried to find out just how loud I had to shout to scare up an echo and then how loud they needed to be to get more than one repetition.

My courage grew another size, and I wanted to stand in the canoe to get a better view over the bank. After a few tries, I learned to stand without upsetting the boat. Then I bounced the canoe up and down. Soon I was rocking the boat side to side.

I talked to cows. "I'm the law," I shouted. "I say what goes around here. You don't do what I say . . . well . . . I won't shoot ya 'cause I don't shoot anybody. But I'll find someone to shoot ya."

I sang Gene Autry's "Back in the Saddle Again."

In a high-pitched Slim Pickens impression, I screeched, "Billy Bob broke the back of Bulgin' Bill's bovine."

I held my fingers out like guns and shot at the cows: "I guess I will shoot ya. Bang! Bang! Bang! You silly sumbitches." I slapped the paddle on the water and sent more sharp cracks echoing down the river.

None of it impressed the livestock.

After all that yelling and screaming, the silence was loud. Only the sound of the wind in the pines drifted down the river. I leaned back into the stern and turned my face up into the sun. I had never felt freer. Whatever home turned out to be, I thought, life had to be easier and better than what I left. I felt confident. I felt grand.

The river widened to between 100 and 150 yards. The wind blew in puffs, and the water often ran smooth as a mirror. My boat and I floated in a patch of the sky—bottomless pale blue. Rushes spread in swaths along the lee bank and gave way to grass and sagebrush upland. Small groves of cottonwoods grew along the banks; and where the river coursed wide and slow, aspens and birch filled in between the cottonwoods. Over the course of the day, the bluffs stepped away from the banks. Grassy meadows rose gently to the foothills beyond. The floodplain broadened, and the pines that grew on the hills gave way to prairie grass.

The river was my friend. It pulled the boat along without any effort from me. Forced up in the current, sand brushed the bottom of the boat. Swallows twittered and water splashed against the cut bank. I nodded off a few times but fought the urge to fall into deep sleep.

Late in the afternoon the sky clouded over, but the breeze stayed easy. Despite my efforts, I went to sleep. I was dreaming pleasantly when a wave hit the side of the boat and rocked it up violently. I opened my eyes to a dark sky and cold wind. Half awake, I jostled into my seat and fumbled for the paddle. Gusts of wind busted down the river, raising foamy waves and spray over the bow. A gray opaque curtain of rain pressed forward from downstream, swallowing the hills and river bottoms as it went. Stiff wind forced the boat one direction, then the other. Lightning flashed; thunder rolled in sharp echoing claps.

That feeling I had of being an expert canoeist deserted me; the new, confident man melted away as the curtain fell. I bumped down onto my knees and paddled in long deep strokes. Not knowing what to do or where to take the boat, I chided myself for getting complacent. Isn't it just like me, I said to myself, to think a few calm and easy moments meant that everything was just fine and would be forever?

Floating in the middle of the Missouri in a lightning storm seemed like a very bad idea. Panic set in. To the right rose a fifteen-foot-high cut bank. Grass roots atop the bank snapped like whips. To the left, the swollen river ran up into a cottonwood grove. On backpacking trips in Wyoming and Missouri, I had seen storms uproot whole cottonwood trees. Cottonwoods didn't appeal to me in that moment. The cut bank offered no shelter.

What to do? Pant, pant. Which way to go?

The sky closed completely, and darkness as deep as night descended on the river. Rain whipped my face and arms in stinging sheets. The wind pushed the boat upstream sideways. The rain and darkness limited my vision to just a few yards. My glasses fogged over. Streams of water ran down into my eyes. Waves splashed over the bow and sides of the boat.

When lightning flashed, I could see the cut bank. A sagebrush bush teetered on the lip at the top of the bank, and its roots thrashed in the space below. I shook the water from my eyes and paddled for that bank. But I lost sight of it as the wind turned my boat again. Lightning lit the sky in an eerie green glow. Every flash froze waves and suspended sheets of rain and splashes of river water in the air until another lightning flash captured it all a little differently. Thunder shook the boat and rumbled into my chest. Soon the lightning flashes and thunderclaps were simultaneous.

"Shit-shit-goddammit-shit!" I screamed into the rain.

Are you my friend now? I thought. Do I let you take me where you want?

I ached for solid ground.

Hail the size of peas fell. Another lighting flash revealed a tangle of willows that stuck out into the current on the lee bank. A cottonwood grove rose just beyond. Trees would catch the lightening first. Being so near them, I would get it as well. But what the hell? I paddled toward those willows with everything I had. If the wind worked against one side of the canoe, I muscled water on the other. The hail grew to the size of marbles. It pelted my head and shoulders in painful whacks.

I crashed into the willows and wrapped a wad of the slim branches around one of the canoe's cross braces to hold the boat in place. The hail stung like hornets. I ripped open one of my bags, yanked out a bath towel, and bent down over my knees. I pulled the towel over my head and shoulders to soften the hail's blow. I cursed. I doubted. I was cold. I scrunched into a tight ball against the storm. The hail grew bigger, and the rain fell in heavier sheets. Beneath it all, the river roared.

A branch as long and as big around as a telephone pole snapped off the tree above and splashed into the water next to the boat. A wave sloshed into the canoe. Sticks and leaves fell with the rain. I yelled curses, if only to hear my own voice over the roar of the storm.

After what seemed an age, the lightning grew sporadic. The hail became smaller and stopped. The wind let up, and the rain turned into a steady pour.

I eased up out of my ball. I felt light, almost weightless, after all the crash and bang. I was cold, my neck and back stung from the hail, but I wasn't injured. The canoe, with nearly two inches of hail in the bottom, was like a big bucket of agates and pearls. They rolled against my ankles. I took up handfuls and turned the stones over in my hand. The colors changed as the sky went from green black to gray and then to blue within minutes. I was glad to be whole.

As the storm passed, I pulled back out into the river and bailed the hail out with a tiny pan from my mess kit. Around the next bend, only a third of a mile from that knot of willows, the bridge crossed the river into Ulm. I was so close! I felt silly and relieved. I stood in the boat like a gondolier. I laughed. I cracked the paddle on the river's surface and bounced the boat. I whooped and screamed and broke into hysterics.

I sloshed out of the boat and wobbled over to a park bench. Evening orange settled over the farmland and the prairie. A full rainbow spread against dark clouds racing upstream. The river and the far bank melted into a wide plain that rose into dark mesas in the distance. The sun was low to the horizon. It disappeared behind a cloud, and the sky broke into a hundred rays of orange and red. Whatever I wanted to do could wait.

After a long time a breeze came up and gave me a chill. I changed and wrung out my sopping clothes. Fresh and dry, I pitched my tent in deep, wet grass. When I was finished, I walked on sea legs into Ulm, a two-road town next to I-15 where I found a phone and called my daughter.

"It's nice," she said when I asked her about the weather in Kansas City. She had been playing with friends and wanted to get back to her games. Her world was far from mine, and our phone call gave me some perspective. My harrowing adventure belonged to me, an accident of a thunderstorm sweeping across the plains. It wasn't so important in the larger scheme of things. Except for the branch breaking off the cottonwood, the storm probably presented less danger than I thought. I wondered what might have happened if I had just quit fighting and let the boat float without my direction. I felt fantastic.

On the way back to the park, I walked past a sheriff's deputy sitting in his prowler at the side of the road.

"I've just come in off the river," I said to him through the open passenger window. "I'd like to stay at the park there by the bridge. But the signs say no overnight camping."

"You don't have a car?" he said.

"Nope," I said. "I've come from Wolf Creek in a canoe."

"Well, climb in, and I'll call the station and let them know you're here."

As soon as I sat down in the passenger seat, he demanded my driver's license. I carried it with my phone card, or I would have left it with my other gear. He radioed his dispatcher.

"You're checking what right now?" I said. I felt I was being pushed around.

"To see if you're legal," he said.

"You could've told me," I said.

"That you're legal?" he said.

"That you were running my license like I'd committed a crime," I said.

"Yeah, but I'm a cop," he said. "I don't have to tell you much of anything."

I fumed. He gave me my license back. I slammed the door of the car and stomped back toward camp. He pulled the patrol car up next to me.

"Sorry, buddy," he said. "I didn't mean nothing by it."

"Am I legal?"

"Yeah," he said. "We don't have anything on you."

"Will I have to leave the park?" I said.

"No, not at all," he said. "You enjoy your stay. There'll be another deputy drive by to check on you later."

"He'll call me in too?" I said.

"Come on," he said. He adjusted his flat-brimmed hat. "I said I was sorry."

"Thanks . . . buddy."

As I walked back to the park, my anger faded into fatigue. I didn't much like Officer Friendly's calling in my number. But I was tired. I started a small fire, made a dinner of pasta and olive oil, and wrote and dozed at the picnic table. Thunderstorms. Cops. Hail. Elation. Terror. Doubt.

Later, another deputy pulled up to the locked gates of the park.

"Patrick," he shouted. He stood at the side of his prowler, waving. "Mr. Dobson!" He was a young man, trim and muscular, in a pressed uniform. I could see his smile from two hundred feet away. "You all right in there?"

I felt my brow scrunch, eyes narrow, and lips tighten. "Different cop," I told myself. I tucked my dented ego away and walked over to him. We shook hands. The skin of his hand was soft; and his face, unblemished pink. His teeth were perfect.

"Thanks for looking in on me," I said. "Please tell the other deputy I'm sorry for being a jerk."

"Well," he said, "he wanted me to tell you he's sorry for not handling the situation better. Well, he said he treated you 'like a dick.' His words. I'm sorry too. Cascade County's pretty nice, and Ulm's usually a friendly town. I hope you don't hold it against us and come back sometime."

Imagine that, I said to myself.

Toward sunset mice rustled in the grass and skittered across bare spots of red gravel around my picnic table. The plains dominated the landscape, the foothills retreating in waves behind me. Across the river and downstream, fields of grass and wildflowers swayed in the breeze. The air was cool and fresh.

A kind of satisfaction set in. I hadn't shot my mouth off and gotten myself arrested. I didn't have to swim my "craft" ashore or rely on my lifejacket to save me, as my canoe instructor Reg was so convinced I would. My gear was safe. The boat held rock steady. It had taken the waves and wind well, a good thing for as panicky as I was.

Except for the rapids the previous day and the thunderstorm, the river had taken it easy on me. There had been a few sweepers along my way, but the biggest threats had been nothing more than sticks. I hadn't encountered underwater hazards. And from what I could divine, I wasn't rolling around in the water below a diversion dam. Days and days of hair-raising episodes might lay ahead, but I couldn't know for sure.

I took in the quiet, intense, and beautiful landscape. As the sun squeezed into the horizon, I thought of my brother. As kids, we sometimes stood barefoot at the backyard fence in the springtime and watched the sun set. The color and the light entranced us until the last of the sun disappeared behind the houses on the next street over. Mom called us to dinner sometimes, waking us from our reverie. It was then we realized our hands had cramped from holding the fence wire and our feet were cold. We'd look at each other and wonder how we got there. We headed inside the house without a word.

We were both little then, and it was probably the only peace we ever knew together. Our home life was difficult, often violent and arbitrary. Our dad—bless him—drank too much and meted out harsh punishment. Later in life my brother and I both beat ourselves in storms of our own making. When I started drinking, I drew away from family until I didn't know them anymore. He went his way, and I mine. When we meet today, we are strangers who want to bridge chasms so dangerous and difficult to cross we don't dare try. Someday, maybe.

When I think of that sunset today, I see tiny Ulm turning on its lights. The headlights on I-15 sweep in slow arcs through the landscape as if through a dream. It's getting dark. The sky grows bigger, until it's filmy with stars. I feel the river out there in the dusk. It flows without a sound around two kids standing barefoot at a fence, sharing wordlessly what they might look a lifetime to find again.

6   Medicine River

AFTER ULM THE RIVER WIDENED AND USHERED ME THROUGH its valley with a gentleness I have only known a few times in my life. Traumas of the previous day faded into distant memories. As I floated, I wondered if the Missouri, my sometime friend, thrashed me the day before for fun or out of anger. Could a river even be angry, happy, or sad? Did the river exist on its own or express nature itself? Did it matter? Regardless, I assumed, the river gave little thought to me. It lived its own life, and I was part of it, nothing more.

I drifted in an endless ribbon of sky. The land rolled away from it into a series of low, grass-covered hills. Sandbars grabbed hold of the boat, but I overcame them with a few easy strokes and resumed my daydreams. Plovers, sandpipers, and gulls strutted along sandy beaches. Immense flocks of white pelicans, having found sandbars just beneath the river's surface, looked as though they stood on the water in the distance. Cormorants flew in so close that I saw their orange faces and blue eyes. They fluttered across the water and gathered in pairs and groups of three and four, sometimes swimming by the boat just within my reach.

After a while, I slipped into thoughts of people at home. Little anxieties — unfinished business, responsibilities I disregarded, bad memories — bubbled into my consciousness. They produced twinges of remorse that grew into regret. Members of my family and those of Sydney's mother had accused me of running off without considering anyone's needs but my own. I feared for Sydney. She needed a father who stayed close, gave her assurance, and guided her through childhood. I was a distracted dreamer who couldn't sit still and work a steady job. The thought of expecting another adventure, first in the Great Plains and now on the river, to change my world made me restless. I distracted myself with reading. But after a while, this didn't keep me from falling into self-recrimination. I climbed into my seat and paddled as hard as I could. Within a few seconds, the canoe left a wake down the middle of the river. Soon, I breathed hard and broke a sweat.

I could give myself all the reasons and excuses for going on this trip: I needed a challenge and believed such a test made up for lost time. I wanted something to write about. I needed to know myself. I wanted to show my kid that life offered more than working and dying. None of these, however, changed the fact that I'd run off, left my daughter, and saddled her mom with immense responsibility. This wandering around the landscape and into other people's lives might only wreak havoc and bring me no salvation.

I paddled harder.

One measures the injury a drunk does not in their sickness and self-destruction but in the relationships they break, cars they wreck, and property they destroy. In my drinking past, I had ruined friendships and alienated and hurt people. I had been headstrong. I had lied, stolen, and cheated. I indulged in sharp practices. I made bad business deals and borrowed money that I never paid back. Giving no regard to well-meaning women, friends, and family who cared about me, I was needy and demanding. I bullied people around or took advantage of them depending on what I wanted. I had lived in a blackout and had no idea of the extent of the wrongs I'd perpetrated. How could I right them when I didn't even know half of the debris I'd left in my wake?

I took it out on myself, as if muscle ache and joint pain punished me aptly for having been so thoughtless and egotistical. I was in decent shape at the time. My back, the size of a zip code, has always been strong. I sunk that strength into the water. My shoulders swiveled on my back. I bent at the waist and heaved at the paddle, as if to dig a hole in the river. Miles flew by. The banks blurred at the periphery of vision centered on myself and growing narrower by the minute.

Panting, my muscles burning, I couldn't escape the shame and regret. Feeling angry and helpless, I started to cry. I told myself I was worthless, that I would never amount to anything. Why should I even try?

Who knows how long I struggled like that? At some point, I dashed the paddle down in the boat and screamed obscenities into the steep hills that had risen on either side of the river without my noticing. I tore my journal out of my bag and began scribbling out letters I intended to post as soon as I found a mailbox. In a fury, I scrawled and scratched away. I confessed to wrongs and took blame. I pleaded for pity and forgiveness. I wrote of betrayals and infidelities, lustful thoughts and angry words, the disappointments I'd been to some and my overblown expectations for others. I swore I was going to be different when I got home. Reformed. I would put my head down. I'd live and work and die like any other human being. I wasn't going to be special anymore.

The boat stuck on sandbars sometimes, I guess for up to an hour before it unstuck itself. Pressing pen so firmly, I scrapped letters and started again because I ripped the paper. One letter was to my daughter's mom. I addressed another four to former girlfriends, women for whom I had longing feelings of want and regret. The opera singer. The German girl. A young artist. A restaurateur I'd dated for a long time. I wrote letters to employers and wanted to make restitution for packs of cigarettes, bottles of wine, or six-packs of beer, as well as food, office supplies, and gasoline. I knew I never stole from a cash register. Instead, I thieved what I'd need money to buy and took things I couldn't afford. A boss might not discover a bottle of liquor I snatched off the shelf for weeks, and then he or she wrote it up as general loss. A pizza or sandwich filched out the back door dissolved into food costs. I operated knowing that finding guilty parties disrupted the workplace — and if there was anything business owners hated more than missing money, it was inefficiency and disruption. Devious stuff. Plain wrong.

I understand in hindsight the selfishness I indulged in that day on the river. I had affected the lives of others. I knew that. I grasped the weight of the damages I'd done. But in writing those letters, I came after myself with a vengeful judgment that I never levy on others. I thought only of myself as I tried to dig the river out of its bed. Other people didn't walk around all day thinking about me. I wasn't that important.

After awhile, pen on paper eased my zeal for mortification of body and mind. Drained, I settled back into the rear of the canoe and watched the hills go by. It was evening and still plenty warm. The river slowed and broadened to over a half mile. The channel disappeared. I had just begun to take a deep breath after getting so overwrought, when, another bend later, as if on cue, the Missouri erupted into a riot of motorboats. Skiers waved as their boat drivers splashed up for a look at the canoe. Wakes crashed against wakes and worked the water into standing waves and angry haystacks. Sometimes the chop grew worse than I encountered during the thunderstorm the day before. At one point a large cabin cruiser skimmed the water toward me. I turned the canoe and the boat followed. As I tried to decide which way to jump, the boat spun in a tight arc and sprayed me with water. Its wake busted up against the canoe. I retreated for the bank and out of the path of recreation. I soon found that sticking close to the bank prevented the Jet Skis and motorboats from swooping in for a closer look.

I laughed. I didn't need to beat myself up. Great Falls would do it for me.

Meanwhile, the town appeared at first in trailer homes and small houses near the riverbank. Downstream, these gave way to larger suburban houses on trim lawns carved into the sagebrush hills. In town, hardwoods shaded bungalows on sleepy streets that seemed far removed from the noise on the water. Near the center of town, I beached the canoe in the willows at the riverfront park.

I dropped my life vest into the canoe and climbed the bank. Picnic tables and grills stood under the trees, and a few families sat on the grass on blankets. The park was neat and quiet under the cottonwoods and sycamores. I laid in the grass with the world rocking below me. After I got my legs back, I fetched my stove and supplies for dinner and dined extravagantly on piles of noodles, onions, summer sausage, and dried fruit.

Toward dusk water traffic slowed. One by one, boats and Jet Skis whooshed out of the chaos and into orderly lines at the public dock and boat ramp. Cars and trucks backed trailers into the water and drove their boats away. Soon the park was nearly empty and the water quiet. A few lovers and people with dogs strolled down the sidewalks, and lights began to appear in house windows. I spread my sleeping bag on the grass near a picnic table and was soon dreaming of people from my past. They grimaced and screamed. Boats and skiers and dams ripped the canoe from beneath me, and I sank into the black depths.

At 6:00 a.m. sprinklers popped up next to my head and splashed me out of this uneasy sleep. Stumbling and dragging my sleeping bag behind me, I made for dry ground. The sun was coming up and traffic began to move along the thoroughfare next to the park. Garbage trucks beeped as they backed up to dumpsters, city trucks grumbled slowly along the street, and work crews emptied park trashcans and mowed grass. I ached for proper coffee and abandoned my things on a picnic table in the sun to search for a coffee house.

Still unsure of myself, I needed more information about getting around the dams and the falls. At a little café near the park, the woman behind the counter let me use a phone and phone book. I called various outdoors and canoeing stores to find a canoeing club or at least someone who knew about these things. Several failed attempts later, I accepted the idea of canoeing down to the Montana Power hydroelectric facility and taking what came. But I made one more call and the man on the phone gave me the names of Starla and Alan Rollo, members of the Medicine River Canoe Club.

Over the phone Starla offered to find someone to take me downstream, around the hydroelectric dams and the last of the falls. Instead of sleeping in the park another day, I should feel myself welcome to use the guest room in her basement. She didn't listen to my protest and met me at the park an hour later in a big red Suburban. We lifted the boat and set it on the car's roof rack. She secured the canoe to the car with stout ropes and complicated knots. She smiled when she stood back from her work.

"How long have you been canoeing?" she said. She was quiet and shy. She never looked me in the eye but instead gazed askance at my shoulder or at my knees.

"About three days," I said.

"No, I mean overall, not just on the Missouri," she said.

"Well, I've pretty much only been in a canoe since I got on the Missouri three days ago."

"No kidding," she said. "That's something. It's a big river. I haven't been canoeing long, but my husband's been in it for a long time. From what he's shown me, I think the Missouri's a great river. You'll enjoy it.

"But you don't want anything to do with Morony Rapids. That's where Montana Power'll drop you off. That's something for someone with a little more experience, I think. I've only ever seen them, and that's enough for me. We'll get you a little farther along somehow."

"But I don't want to put you out," I said. "I'm just a stranger to you."

"Oh, that's all right. There's something about you I trust."

I found myself feasting again at a stranger's table, receiving another gift I couldn't return. Years before, when I was drunk and living from paycheck to paycheck, I relied on people to give me all kinds of things, from a simple meal to small change when I came up short at a cash register. I started a river trip without experience. I wondered if I expected, in the back of my head, as I headed out, that strangers would get me through.

On the drive to her house, I stared out the window, watching the river. At the bridge past the public boat ramp, the river fell some three feet over a cliff in the rock bottom. The speed of the current increased as it approached the dam. It gave me the willies.

"You don't want a thing to do with that either," Starla said, as if reading my mind.

Starla took me to lunch and, later, put me up in a comfortable bedroom in her basement, where I napped for a long time. After her husband came home, we had a sumptuous dinner. They were young and strong, windswept in a healthy, glowing way. We talked about river journeys, discoveries you make on them, and lessons you learn on the way. I teetered off to bed and stared into the drop ceiling a long time. Given how bad I felt the day before, I wondered how I came into this. I felt safe. Starla and Alan wanted nothing from me and gave to a stranger the way I would have. They treated me well for no other reason than they could. Would they do this for just anyone? Would it have been different had I been black or Native American? Did such things matter to them? Starla said there was something about me she trusted. What did that mean?

When I came upstairs the next morning, Starla had already cooked breakfast. Alan was off to work. We were drinking coffee when Jim and Dianne McDermand arrived. Starla had called them the previous evening, and I guessed the Rollos schemed up a plan for me while I was sleeping.

Over the course of two decades, the McDermands paddled rivers all over the state of Montana north of Great Falls and into Canada. They founded the Medicine River Canoe Club to advocate canoeing for relaxation and sport. Jim and Dianne were older than my hosts. Jim was a big man, burly, with wide shoulders and large hands. Dianne was small and petite but wiry and powerful. She was determined and outgoing; Jim, more quiet and introspective. They finished each other's sentences and were not shy about their opinions. They were more conservative than I am, but we shared strong feelings about the environment and conservation. Because we didn't agree on everything, we had spirited discussions over just how far people and government should go to manage or preserve the environment.

I fell in with the Rollos and McDermands at the right time. My guilty feelings of the previous day evaporated. These people offered help to anyone who had anything to do with the Missouri. I was glad of it. In Kansas City months before, information I'd gained about canoeing the Missouri ranged from sketchy to negative. One man at a local canoe club told me I would be lucky to make ten to fifteen miles a day working hard. Most of the time, he said, "You'll make five or six miles. I hope you planned enough time." I had paddled over seventy miles in three days. Another Kansas Citian, known locally for his canoeing skill, droned on about waves, wind, and impossible portages around dams. I asked how he knew. He said he had no experience in such matters. He just knew.

Fortunately, my new patrons really understood the river, and I hung on their every word.

"You don't want anything to do with Morony Rapids," Dianne said, and I couldn't help but smile, wondering if Dianne hadn't gotten this from Starla, or vice versa. "It's whitewater for four miles, with large drops and rapids. I've done it. Jim's done it. But you shouldn't, not with your experience. We could take you to Carter, a little town just past all that, but the stretch from there to Fort Benton is tedious and boring.

We'll get you right to Fort Benton tomorrow. That'll be good for you and a nice trip for us."

We went to the backyard, and they looked through my equipment, which Jim said "wasn't bad for an amateur." I told him how I packed and how I was learning quickly about canoeing.

Dianne went over my boat while Jim and I talked.

"You're pointing the bow of your boat forward?" Dianne exclaimed.

"Sure," I said. "How else?"

"My friend," she said confidingly as she reached up and patted me on the shoulder, "when you solo in a canoe, you put the stern forward. Since the front seat sits farther from the bow than the back seat does from the stern, you'll sit more toward the center of the boat. It'll be easier to balance yourself and your gear. Who told you otherwise?"

I didn't tell her about the canoe lesson with the Blond Hourglass in Helena.

Dianne and I drove around Great Falls while Jim attended to canoe-club business elsewhere. At a bookstore, we picked up a couple of how-to canoeing manuals and a copy of Bernard Devoto's *The Journals of Lewis and Clark*. After all, she argued, if I was trailing the Corps of Discovery, I should know something of the expedition. Next door, I bought a fine straw hat in the shape of a pith helmet, with a drawstring under the chin. She was enthusiastic and encouraged me. She dismissed the myths and horror stories. No whirlpool would swallow my boat. Catfish didn't pull paddlers to the depths. Beyond Morony, no falls, rapids, or diversion dams crossed my path. Weather would be what it was. I should exercise caution, she said, but never be fearful.

"The river is your friend," she said.

"Especially if I don't fight it," I said.

"Yes," she said. "That's exactly right. It'll be hard to remember sometimes. But it's good insight. You've learned a lot already."

The next afternoon, we arrived in Fort Benton. I bought waterproof river maps from the Upper Missouri National Wild and Scenic River visitor's center. These charted the territory from Fort Benton into the Charles M. Russell National Wildlife Refuge and Fort Peck Reservoir. Jim, Dianne, and I spent most of the afternoon and evening walking along the river and talking. We ended the day in the riverfront park. We took turns reading literature on the Missouri out loud to each other. They left at dusk, and I was sad to see them go.

I lit my candle lantern and read the letters I'd written two days before. I had forgotten them while I was in Great Falls and hadn't posted them. I was glad about it when I realized just how selfish those notes were. Actually, I was embarrassed. In them, I whined and pleaded. I wrote as if I knew how others felt about me—an arrogance, I've found, that accompanies low self-esteem. Worse, the letters showed I believed I could right years of bad behavior in an hour or a day. A couple of the people I had written to were, at best, distant acquaintances. In all likelihood, they wouldn't have even remembered me.

I kept those letters. I read them today and see that they could not have repaired my past. They might have made some injuries worse. I had just begun a process that would progress one bite, one step, one minute at a time. Since my journey, I have spoken with some of the people I wrote to that day and have made amends. I contacted places I worked and came to monetary agreements for the goods I stole. But in the end, nothing was as big a deal as I wanted it to be. That day on the river, I wanted to be forgiven and sought absolution. It wasn't going to come in one magical trip. I'm still at this work today.

I find it fortunate, too, that I fell into deep self-pity when I did. The morning after the McDermands dropped me off in Fort Benton, I headed into a stretch of the Missouri where I would be more alone than any other time in my life.

7   A Speck in the Landscape

BEFORE I STARTED THE CANOE TRIP, MY IDEA OF THE RIVER hinged on disconnected impressions: My father and I watched the river from a rocky bank, my hand in his. I caught glimpses of it from bridges and riverside highways. A flooded Main Street appeared on the television news, or a boat wreck showed up in black-and-white photographs on the front pages of the newspaper. The river frightened me as much as it intrigued me. In the pages of books, I rafted with Tom Sawyer and Huck Finn. I explored the continent with Lewis and Clark and performed mythic feats of survival with John Coulter and William Henry Ashley and his intrepid mountain men. In graduate school, I traveled up the river with Prince Maximilian von Wied-Neuwied and his painter-companion Karl Bodmer. Over and over, I flipped through the pages of Maximilian's journals illustrated with Bodmer's work, imagining myself on the river, seeing in person the river Bodmer showed me. His paintings and illustrations captivated me and, ultimately, influenced my decision to canoe the river home from Montana.

The Missouri River I felt in my paddle, the one that ran over my feet and through my fingers, matched little the river of my imagination. I was no longer a scared child at my father's side, staring with incomprehension at the spectacle before me. The river of Mark Twain, Lewis and Clark, and the fur trade mattered not at all. The river flowed stronger than in Bodmer's sketches and paintings. Witnessing the storm and letting the Missouri's sinewy current wrap about my body, I'd discovered in the river a life that was its own. It was harsh. It didn't forgive. At the same time, it was sublime and gentle, welcoming. Despite the surprises and dangers, I continued down the river. I wanted to see what it would give me next.

The Missouri possessed a subtle beauty at Fort Benton that it did not have above Great Falls. The magnificent craggy bluffs along the river above the falls gave over to brown grass along the banks. That brown turned blond as the land rose to low, rounded hills in the distance. A slower, gentler river, it was also warmer and more opaque. Sheets of light skipped off the water and made me blink and squint. Flocks of pelicans grew larger and laid across the water like fluttering white expanses that broke into a thousand pieces and took to the sky at my approach. The pines disappeared. The breezes now carried the odors of dust and sagebrush off the plains. The river smelled of equal parts slow creek, cold-water spring, and fish. They mingled together into a delicious heavenly scent that I decided not to take for granted.

I put the canoe on the water and stepped into that space between heaven and earth. As I paddled away from Fort Benton, human sounds — cars, trucks, the bangs and rattles of freight — faded away. The river flowed here between six hundred and a thousand feet wide. It eased the boat around wide arching curves and tight bends. Willows and cottonwoods filled squarish cuts in the banks that marked the river's former channels. The bottoms were green with sagebrush, and willows spread along the bank. Chutes and narrow watery pathways wound behind numerous islands. In places, the river slowed almost to a standstill. Once again, I found myself adrift not on water but on the very blue of heaven itself.

Cupping my hands, I splashed water over my head against the heat. The river tasted good, and I filled one of my bottles with my pack water purifier. The cool water splashed down through the hollow of my chest. The river held a personality without, which I felt pleasantly within. I wondered just how separate I was from it.

I took Dianne McDermand's advice and turned the stern of my boat forward. The canoe responded more quickly to my paddle. I used my five-gallon water bag to adjust for the wind. Pushed to the front, the bag, some forty pounds or more when full, weighed the nose down and made the boat easier to steer in a headwind. When the wind blew from behind, I moved the bag toward me and sometimes even behind me and made the back of the boat sit lower in the water. When the breeze died down, I moved the bag to the center and put miles behind me with less effort. When it came time to read or nap, I gave up moving the bag around and let the canoe wander where it might.

Toward afternoon, waves rolled upstream against the current, as if the wind were peeling off the river's skin. I moved in close to shore and kept an eye out for good landing places in case things got rough. Soon the wind howled off the plain, and I headed face first into it. For a while, I paddled in rhythm with the splash of waves against the bow. My head emptied. Nothing existed but water, sun, and sky. When the wind grew too strong, I took to the bank and waited it out. There were few signs of humans here, just river, willows, sagebrush, and grassy hills. I laid down in the grass in the sun and slept soundly.

The wind died suddenly, waking me up. The water smoothed out quickly, and I soon canoed past the Marias River near Loma. The Marias coursed nearly as wide as the Missouri, and a large island swung away from the confluence. Wetlands and stands of willows covered the river bottom. With the Marias now, the Missouri grew bigger shoulders and widened to nearly a thousand feet. Its currents were stronger, though it was still often broad and slow. It flowed in a magnificent gully in the plains above. Turf curled off the high cut banks; the lee banks rose from the water slowly and in profusions of willow saplings and water grasses. Wildflowers bloomed in hundreds of colors. Cottonwoods now covered islands and some of the floodplain. Cormorants and ducks played in eddies off the tail ends of islands. Carp scattered in splashes and large swells at the prow of the boat.

About twenty miles from Fort Benton, I hauled my canoe up away from the bank, turned it over, and tied it to a sturdy tree. This, I hoped, would keep it from blowing away in a stiff wind. I checked my knots and trusted they would hold. Beavers had chewed through all the saplings and small trees here. I hoped they'd leave the seats and thwarts in the canoe alone.

My camp, set on a grassy notch in a hill about a hundred yards from the river, commanded a broad view across the valley. The river flowed like a long mirror in the green-carpeted bottoms and brown hills. Not one man-made structure or road cluttered my sight. I sat at the edge of the notch and watched as dark clouds rose in plumes on the horizon. They transformed the river into a black ribbon of unimaginable depth. This was the river that flowed silently behind those fields of wheat I'd dreamed about at night on the walk to Helena. Now, however, it wasn't a silent and unseen presence at the edges of dreams but a clear path leading somewhere. I didn't yet know exactly where.

Living out in the open does peculiar things to me. With the sun as my guide, time just doesn't matter. I find myself again in the shoes of my youth, when I could stare into a fire or at a sunset for hours without a thought to anything else. Sunrise and sunset direct my days. Without electric lights illuminating a day that I make, I wake with the dawn and become sleepy after the sun sets. I talk to myself, laugh at my own jokes, and carry on long monologues. Everything—from the tiniest cricket crawling through the grass to the sound of the wind in the leaves—rises to the level of consciousness. I hear myself breathe. My heart beats in my ears. I feel who I am inside.

Hours passed as I sat next to my tent and watched the river. Cloud shadows raced across the landscape until the sun fell low to the horizon and the sky began to close. After it grew overcast, two people in an inflatable raft eased through the dark-green-and-brown countryside. I was sure they didn't notice me on my grassy ledge. It was unendingly peaceful to watch them. I wondered who they were and what they were looking for. I thought of my daughter and what she might be up to and just how distant this world was from hers.

Night fell. It was raining steadily when I crawled into the tent. I lit the candle lamp and read the Lewis and Clark journals. The sound of the rain and wind on the canvas soon put me to sleep.

During the night, storms rolled off the plains. Thunder boomed up the valley and sounded like drums in a huge, empty room. The rain started in earnest and, with the wind, bowed my small tent inward. Lightning repeatedly struck close to my camp and made the ground shake. Before the trip to Montana, I experienced lightning simultaneous with thunderclaps only three times: once on the way home from the golf course where I caddied when I was sixteen, once while camping in the Colorado Rockies when I was twenty-four, and once at a city park when I was thirty. Before my trip, I only witnessed lightning striking the ground one time. I was twenty-five, very drunk, and driving in a thunderstorm outside Flagstaff, Arizona. The rain came down so hard I couldn't see but a few yards. Curtains of rain parted for a moment, and lightning hit with an eerie buzz and crack, forming a bright ball where it entered the ground. As I made my way to Montana, thunderstorms caught me out in the open eleven times. During six of those storms, lightning struck so close that the sound and light came at the same time. Lightning hit the ground within fifty yards from me outside Linwood, Kansas, and North Platte, Nebraska. Since my journey through the plains and back on the river, lightning has scared the wits out of me numerous times on backpacking trips and walks around town. None of it, however, has ever startled or frightened me like standing in a thunderstorm on the plains.

I love it and would rather witness it than not. But it's not something a person gets used to.

Each time the lightning struck that night, screams erupted from my chest without any help from me—just as they had when the storm caught me on the river. My ears rang and my heart beat in my throat. I pressed my hands to my ears and closed my eyes tight, and still the screams came. By the time the lightning and thunder rolled away into the distance and the downpour turned into steady rain, I felt drained. My throat hurt. I cried like a school kid.

When it was over, a feeling of helplessness I never felt before washed over me; and strangely, I was content. For the first time since I had arrived in Helena nearly two weeks before, I felt no fear at all. The storm wrung it out of me. I thought about the ease with which the river flowed through the valley with me on it. I opened the tent and poked my nose out into the dark. The wind had stopped. My breath hung in the air. My little tent seemed so tiny and insubstantial. On the road to Montana, and even in the thunderstorm near Cascade, I had only begun to grasp my insignificance in the world. Now I understood. The world and its people didn't work for me or against me. They were indifferent to me. I accepted that. It was all right.

Listening to the rain, I felt a strong presence I could not define. It existed neither inside nor outside me. It was everywhere and nowhere.

I did not try to understand it as God or spirits or the power of nature or anything else. It was larger than any of these human ideas and conceptions. Yet it was as small as the flame on my candle. I may have been suffering fatigue. The sun and heat may have settled into my bones and made me perceive things unreal. But so what? I sensed utter emptiness and fullness without thinking about it, labeling it, or trying to find out what it was. I had never felt such peace before and have only a few times since.

I woke the next morning to absolute quiet. No man-made or natural sounds broke the silence. The air hung chill and wet, clean and clear. Lightning had splintered the cottonwood I'd tied the canoe to. Pieces of the tree were strewn over the canoe and the ground around it. A stripe of bare wood ran the height of the tree remnant that remained.

I found it easy to get on the river. The memory of feeling absolutely empty kept me thinking. My past sins, whatever they were and however deep they went, had not destroyed the world. I'd repair as much damage and chaos as I could, or at least I'd try. I couldn't restore relationships I'd demolished. Damage leaves scars. People remembered. But I was learning from the past. Maybe my next effort at making amends would start new relationships, bring me back in touch with people I cared about, and forge a better future for them and for me. I was a good dad to my daughter and was becoming an even better one. The people I wronged might never forgive me, but I could, someday, forgive myself.

With these thoughts in my head, I paddled sometimes faster, sometimes slower, without break until well into midafternoon. The work felt good. The winds remained calm. The canoe moved from one side of the river to the other, depending on how the current bent around the smooth hills and flanks of long ridges. The breeze ruffled the water and showed me paths between sandbars and shallows. The McDermands told me that the current washed out sandbars from beneath leaving precarious and thin ledges above. I'd read of canoeists and kayakers who fell through these ledges and rolled around under lips of a sandbar for days. Sometimes rescuers found only their life vests and jackets with a perfectly upright canoe nearby.

Soon I discovered how those river travelers died. Despite my effort at reading the water and avoiding sandbars, the boat hung up on one, then another. After running the boat aground and wrestling it free a few times with the paddle, I gave up and climbed shoeless from the canoe to pull or push it free. A sandbar-stuck boat wasn't likely to unstick itself in enough time to satisfy me. I liked the feel of the river. It wrapped gently around my calves. The sand felt good underfoot. Hundreds of river travelers have pulled themselves off sandbars without dying, I reasoned. Only an unlucky few ever wound up in the newspaper. As long as I wasn't stupid—and even if I was—I assured myself that the river was my friend and that I'd only get hurt fighting it. Soon I navigated these bends and pulled the boat free of sandbars with confidence.

I floated into a region of long, rocky ridges. Deep ravines, known as breaks and coulees, cut through a great uplift of sandstone and entered the valley between cliffs of powdery brown. As I moved downstream, the color of the rock turned red and then white and yellow. A seam of coal bled down the faces of the bluffs and steep banks in curtains of bluish black.

In the 1860s a few rugged men and women pounded livings out of that layer of coal. Their business proved spotty and unsure. Steamboats were always energy hungry. Steamboat captains, however, found the coal marginal, at best, for their purposes and only bought it when they found no wood. As often as not, the miners' work seldom paid off. Their effort barely kept them in food and clothes. It didn't help that the river here was cantankerous and unpredictable. Whole bluffs and hillsides slid into the current, upending the miners' work and changing the river's course overnight. When the river wandered, it forced these workers to transport their wares farther and with greater effort.

Miners also competed with woodhawks, who chopped trees at the banks and provided the steamboats with more economical and efficient fuel. Woodhawks fared better because they could chop wood anywhere. If the river moved overnight, they moved with it. Stiff wind tore the limbs off the cottonwoods and washout rain uprooted whole groves of trees, downing the wood for them. But they, too, lived an uncertain existence. The same tornado or flood that made their work easier also created vast fields of hull-piercing snags that steamboat captains would not brave. Rocks, boulders, and sand shifted on the bottom like piles of leaves in a wind. Landslides often blocked the channel and stopped river traffic altogether. What may be a perfect season for steamboats getting trade in and out of the Upper Missouri could, the next day, be a bust.

Coal Banks Landing, a simple square of grass with a boat ramp, stood in a bottom between the ridges where coal miners had attempted to find their fortunes. In the late 1870s, steamboats landed here and delivered supplies to workers building Fort Assiniboine north of the river near Havre, Montana. The army sought a defensive position against attacks by Native Americans from the north, after a force of Arapahos, Lakotas, and Northern Cheyennes routed Custer at Little Big Horn. Sitting Bull and his Hunkpapa Lakotas had fled to Canada just north of the present-day Montana border. The Nez Perces found a home in Alberta. The military installation included tens of thousands of acres of land extending nearly to the Missouri river in the south. The fort itself housed over seven hundred troops in a hundred buildings. But no Native Americans ever invaded from the north, so soldiers trained and sat and waited. The army finally vacated the post in 1916 and ceded a portion of the military reservation to the Chippewa Crees for what was to become the Rocky Boy Indian Reservation.

At Coal Banks Landing, one tree grew in a fenced square of ground behind a sign indicating that the Bureau of Land Management (BLM) maintained the river access and boat ramp. A man and woman fished from their chairs at the bank. I was glad to see human beings. I introduced myself. John and Pat were from Great Falls.

"Well, now, that's the way I've always wanted to travel," John said. Whitish stubble covered his rotund face. His fishing pole was taller than he was. The hook swung around the rod and flipped in his hand.

"Sure, it's great," I said, as I climbed from the boat.

John's face turned sage, know-it-all. His eyes narrowed and closed; his head cocked. He tucked his chin under and to one side. I knew what was coming.

"That Fort Peck Lake is a 150 miles long," he said with a patronizing tone. "That's a lot of water. I know; I worked there for three years. I saw one or two people make it all the way across that lake, but that was it. I wouldn't recommend it for anyone. You get out there in that big water and get stuck . . . why . . ."

"Let's say I make it," I interrupted. "How's getting around the dam?"

"You'll portage a mile and a half or more," he said, as if it were the easiest thing in the world. "You're just going to carry your boat around."

I changed the subject and asked John about himself. He said he was a simple man "of retirement years." He didn't give himself enough credit. He was a young-looking sixty. His wife, Pat, was younger by ten or fifteen years and tall with red curly hair and glasses. They were a good-looking couple. They invited me to a cup of coffee and a sandwich.

We walked up the bank to their camper — a practical and compact trailer with everything a home needs. The day was quiet but for the wind in the grass. A few birds chirped in the tree. I found John and Pat as interesting as they were interested in me. They seemed politically moderate and criticized wealth for wealth's sake. The problem with Montana, Pat said, was that companies and people with a great deal of money exploited and ruined the environment just because they could. John agreed and nodded his head as Pat talked. Gaps in our conversation weren't unpleasant. We just smiled and took in the scenery through the camper's tiny windows.

I asked them what they did for a living. They told me they had been independent insurance adjusters.

"Since Montana doesn't have the population for insurance companies to justify full-time adjusters," Pat said, "they contract with people like us."

"Or they used to," John said. "We're out of the business now. We did all kinds of insurance claims work — home, life, auto, workplace liability . . . everything. We saved enough money over the years to quit working."

"Now, we spend our time watching sagebrush grow," Pat said.

It looked to be true, and it was enviable. Pat and John didn't have a radio in their camper. They had no television. They read books. More than once, I'd met people on the way to Helena who didn't do much but sit and look at the landscape. There was something to watching sagebrush grow, I decided. That contentment was something special.

After a while the river called me on. As I left, they sat under the lone tree next to their camper in their lawn chairs. John tipped his coffee cup up as a goodbye.

The sun broke through the clouds. Tall bluffs, gray and yellow-brown, lined the river. Their grassy tops slid into bare hillsides. At times, black lines of coal bled blue drapes down the brown, yellow, and red bluffs and hills. The region looked untouched, but people had used and abandoned this land. It had been unimaginably difficult to make a living in this harsh environment, where temperatures often dropped to minus twenty in the winter and climbed over a hundred in the summer. The climate was dry; the soil, poor; and most times even the grass and sagebrush hardly grew. Trappers, farmers, miners, and speculators exploited the resources they needed and left the land to the next. Only the weathered cabins in the bottoms showed where they had been.

At Little Sandy Creek, around twenty miles from where I began the day, I stopped to find some tipi rings marked in the BLM history digest. I walked in the dry creek bed up to the flat grassland above the bluffs. There I found the simple circles of rounded stones that once held down the leather tipi covers. If the Native Americans didn't choose this spot for any other reason than the view—grassland to the horizon behind and the jagged river valley below—it was good enough.

I marveled at the rings. In the Midwest, weather claims all neglected and abandoned things in just a short time. Wood rots in rain. Rust and mold are permanent conditions of life. In just a few weeks, plants overgrow tools and toys forgotten in the yard. I've often hiked in the woods of central Missouri and come across crumbling chimneys of settlers' cabins and old houses. Freeze-thaw cycles have turned the house foundations to powder. Grass and ivies snake up the chimneys and into the mortar, if there is any. Age advances quickly. I have gone back to an old homestead I saw a few years before and, instead of a hearth, discovered only ivy-covered humps of stones.

Here, however, the rocks that the Native Americans left in the grass a century before looked as if someone dropped them there just a short time ago—just long enough for the grass to grow between the stones.

Shadows lengthened as the sun fell low to the horizon. All day, I absorbed sights and sounds and felt the wind and water. My head floated as empty as a soap bubble. But for that hour I'd spent with the insurance adjusters in their camper, I had been alone.

Today I am glad I found the insurance adjusters. Pat and John were nice people. They acted on me like the tipi rings. They anchored me and my thoughts and gave me perspective on myself. When thoughts of that particular time on the river roll through my mind, I can't help but see two smiling and happy people, a camper, and a tree. It's almost as if they, like the tipi rings, are apparitions or markers of the long past. They bring into focus all the land and river, where I was then and how far I had to go. They make clear just how far I've come.

8 Spirits of the Dead

IN HELENA MY FRIEND GORDON TOLD ME I WASN'T A "COLUMBUS." When I asked him what he meant, he said that I wasn't the kind of person who thought he discovered something for humankind. I was the first person to see what my journey revealed to me, personally. I wasn't asking Native Americans for the eternal secrets of the earth and humanity. As Gordon put it, I wasn't after "magical, mystical Indian juju." I was, he said, exploring my own insides.

Before I left Kansas City, an old friend told me she knew for over a year that I was leaving on a long journey, even before I did. She said she'd seen the restlessness in me before I left on other journeys. She knew I would take off. She just didn't know when or where I'd go.

"You have done this before," she said. "Germany. All those long trips on trains and in cars. When you go wandering in the woods or the desert or out there on the plains, you always go alone. It's never with anyone else. Let me tell you something I don't think you've figured out yet: People don't travel by themselves because they want a good time. They say they want to see the world, meet new people, or whatever. Blah, blah. They're lying. They're looking for themselves."

I remember what she said as I think about my journey now. I ached to experience something different, exotic, and strange. I saw the trip as part escape, part challenge. I sought release from the things that bothered me. Routine crushed me and fatherhood terrified me. The journey would relieve me of my burdens and renew my spirit. I would prove myself—to me, to my child, to the illusive "them." Like pulling a rabbit out of a hat or reappearing in a different room, I'd gain confidence and be the perfect father. At the end of my path, I'd find a new life.

But Gordon and my friend in Kansas City were right. The river offered no salve or balm for what ailed me. It revealed, instead, the ordinary, commonplace me.

The day after I left the insurance adjusters at Coal Banks Landing, I floated into the White Cliffs region of the Upper Missouri. Bleached sandstone bluffs and buttes jutted from the floodplain and out of hills beyond like fortresses, statues, and monuments. I had first seen these milky-white formations in an encyclopedia hidden in my Catholic grade school's library. When I was a kid, chaos and fear haunted my home life. Nuns, priests, and parents frightened me with sin and damnation. The difference between the ideals of the faithful and their behavior confused me. Putting my nose in books relieved me of the confusion and pain, gave reign to my creative imagination, and allowed me moments of calm. About as big as a janitor's closet and in a hard-to-get-to corner of the school's second floor, the library provided refuge from playground bullies and vagaries of home life. In that tiny room, I lived as a caveman among wooly mammoths, saber-toothed tigers, and hairy ground sloths. I imagined myself among the dinosaurs and behind the wheels of race cars. I flew biplanes and hunted lions. I possessed riches, fame, and power. But rivers intrigued me most—the Amazon, the Nile, the Rhine, the Mississippi, and the Missouri. When I was seven, I read *The Adventures of Tom Sawyer* in just three days, and I swallowed *The Adventures of Huckleberry Finn* in just two days a year later. *Life on the Mississippi* was above my head, but I read it anyway. Then the *Encyclopedia Britannica* gave me my first glimpse of the White Cliffs in an article on the Missouri.

Such wonders! The river in the black-and-white picture wasn't the opaque monster that flowed beneath the Broadway Bridge. It shimmered. It coursed below the mysterious bluffs and reflected the cliffs like a mirror. I thirsted to know where the river came from and where it went. This led me to other books, where I gobbled up stories of explorers, mountain men, and fur trappers. Atlas indexes and fact pages placed the Missouri among the world's great rivers. And pictures! I'd stare at them and daydream of Native Americans. I traipsed wildernesses and steered keelboats upstream behind lines of men with the cordelle over their shoulders.

In high school my interests shifted to other things, mostly drinking.

But my Catholic high school library gave respite from my insecurities, problems, and flaws. One day, when I was a junior, I browsed the stacks and found the journals of Prince Maximilian of Wied-Neuwied, who traveled up the Missouri in 1832. His *Travels into the Interior of North America, during the Years 1832–1834* amazed and captivated me. Illustrated with Carl Bodmer's paintings, the journals brought the Missouri River and its people into focus. As a college student and after, whenever I sought respite from life's drudgeries or the difficulties of being me, I retreated to libraries. I went back to the journals again and again.

The bow of the canoe slid through the gentle waves. All around me, Bodmer's sketches and paintings and Maximilian's descriptions came to life and made me look into memory. As I floated through the White Cliffs, I saw through the eyes of that kid again. I paddled up to Citadel Rock, the subject of my favorite Bodmer painting. The dark stone jutted up out of the riverbank like an ice cream cone dropped on a sidewalk. I touched it, still disbelieving I was here. The rock was cool, and the water flowed translucent beneath us. There, earth met sky and water; and in the river, I saw storm, landscape, and stars.

Within a few miles, the white sandstone bluffs rose right out of the river in columns, chimneys, walls, and roofs. Soon the formations walled in both sides of the river. I eased the boat ashore at Eagle Creek. On the far bank, a long, dark stripe descended from a freestanding arch atop the bluff, making the perfect outline of a sewing needle. I'd first seen Bodmer's painting of the Eye of the Needle as a kid. Seeing it now made my jaw drop. Just downstream stood the massive brown-and-black volcanic dike LaBarge Rock, named for Joseph LaBarge, a legendary steamboat captain who had plied the river from St. Louis to Fort Benton from the 1860s through the 1880s. The black-and-brown stone contrasted with the bluffs, making them seem all the whiter.

Weather made and remade the scene by the minute. Stringy clouds spun through the blue. Shadows raced over the rock and shifted its colors from gray and yellow to hues of brown, and back again. The cliffs transformed chameleonlike in and among the shadows and raw sunlight, undulating, fusing with the river, and separating again.

The river was a silent hole in it all. Holding my breath, I heard only my heartbeat. A hole being nothing is something. I thought that "something" reflected not just the cliffs and light and the land around them. The Missouri was also new as yesterday's rain and as old as creation. Endless in the cycles of evaporation and condensation that married it with land and sky, it coursed with all the water that had flowed on the planet and all that ever would. It began with a tiny spring on Jefferson Peak in the Centennial Mountains in Montana and joined the sea in the Gulf of Mexico. If I let myself open up to it, I could feel those connections and understand that anything that happened to me, within me, and around me altered everything else, even just slightly.

Maybe when I sneezed in a Midtown Kansas City bare-bulb apartment in 1983, it caused a thunderstorm in Montana in 1995.

Do rivers think? Not like people. But I knew the Missouri had life, perhaps even a will. It was sentient without humanlike reason: A force that paid no attention to the acts and structures of human beings. Brute and beautiful. Terrible and gentle. Giving and taking. John Neihardt, author of the famed *Black Elk Speaks*, traveled the river in 1908 in a twenty-foot canoe he named *Atom* and published the narrative of his trip, *The River and I*, in 1910. The river, he wrote, was a "cruel, invulnerable, resistless giant that went roaring down the world with a huge uprooted oak tree in its mouth for a toothpick! This yellow, sinuous beast with hell-broth slavering from its jaws! This dare-devil boy-god that sauntered along with a town in its pocket, and a steepled church under its arm for a moment's toy!" The river moved godlike on the face of the earth as if it had "thunderous seven-league boots." It expressed the earth and its universe and all the things in it. The souls of human beings lived in it, as did their joys and sorrows, their best and worst. It was eternal, and I could watch it running out of the cup of my hand.

The river took me through lonely landscapes. Many people had tried to homestead here. Only a few had eked out a subsistence for more than just a couple of years before cities and other opportunities lured them or their children away. Most of the rest gave up. Their cabins and outbuildings weathered in the river bottoms. Wind and sun contorted wooden cattle troughs and split-log fences. Windmills fell into settlers' graveyards like twisted skeletons. Old pickups rusted in dooryards. Artifacts of heartache, these texts told of flood, drought, and infertile soil. They told the tale of heartless accounting and costs exceeding prices. Where the land was not irrigated and farmed, a few ranchers grazed cattle among the failed farmers' refuse. I have never seen a lonelier sight than a cow grazing at the doorstep of a deserted shack.

The people who lived here left records. They signed their names to deeds. They had birth certificates. Their names mark gravestones. There are tax and death records. They belonged to voluntary associations, fraternal organizations, and church groups. But no piece of paper said who they really were. Even diaries, journals, and letters could not reveal the ways they absorbed the difficulties of growing up, being parents, or having inner lives. They remained, at best, numbers and words on yellowed and flaking paper.

Anonymity disturbed me before I left on the trip. While seeing these things made me reflective and melancholy, I knew more as each day on the river passed that I was one of these people. My name would mean as much to someone in the future as the name on a gravestone in these forgotten cemeteries. An anonymous anybody. I was coming to like that. It reduced my importance and my sense of having to be important. The understanding of my own namelessness in the course of time lifted a great burden from me.

I set camp in the small Bureau of Land Management campground at Eagle Creek. Cottonwoods stood over fire rings and bare tent sites. The evening was still. Clouds slowly thickened downstream. Smoke from my fire rose in a perfect column. I used a tree stump as a writing table, where I set a notebook, my candle, and the medicine bag Gordon gave me. Once in a while, a fish jumped in the water next to the bank, sending silent whorls over the river. A thunderstorm echoed up the valley, and deeper green settled all around as the evening advanced. Soon stars came out in veils and blankets. The Missouri's surface was milky with their reflections. Heat lightning flashed above the river downstream.

I awoke in the morning from dreamless sleep that left me drowsy and dull headed. To clear the fog, I hiked up to the grassy plain behind the campground. The morning light fired the prairie yellow and red. The breeze was gentle; the sky reefed with puffy clouds. Tipi rings and rock cairns dotted the edges of the bluffs. The grass and sage flattened out to the horizon in front of me. Behind, the plain tumbled into winding white hallways and then deeper into narrow defiles below. A deer stood on the naked grassland. At my approach, it looked up and stared a long while before it sprang off across the treeless plain. I took off after it in a fruitless chase. I ran until my legs burned and my sides ached. It disappeared into one of the ravines and left me panting and wide awake.

Eagle Creek dribbled out of a gash in the grassland at the bottom of a snakelike canyon sixty feet deep. At the rim of the canyon, eroded stones formed rock gardens of white spikes and domes. Rounded brown sandstone boulders topped thin columns of white sandstone. The canyon spanned less than thirty feet at the top and narrowed to the width of my shoulders at the bottom. The deep and narrow gap wound around dozens of hairpin turns before opening on the bank of the river. The rains had transformed the black-and-brown clay along the rim into oil-slick mud. I moved carefully toward the edge of the canyon for a closer look, but my feet shot from beneath me. I slid down on my butt, panicking at the thought of falling into the sandstone crevice. Somehow, I flipped over and clawed the mud and rock with my hands and boots, coming to a halt at the canyon's edge. I scrabbled back to the top on all fours and threw a deep, throaty laugh into the canyon. When I caught my breath, I made my way to safe and stable spots below the rim, where I tossed rocks and yawped into the canyon's dark, intestine-like innards.

Back at the riverbank, I washed the mud from my clothes and the blood off my hands. I shoved off and was caught again in that surprising place between the earth, sky, and water. Once the river took hold, I pointed the bow downstream and floated lazily along.

The river was kind. I hardly paddled at all. A stretch of twenty-four miles passed in an easy breath. The eroding plain and cliffs revealed sills and dykes of igneous rock — magma that, millions of years ago, had forced its way up through the sandstone, forming features like Citadel and LaBarge rocks. The river sawed through anything that got in its way. Book-spine walls of blackish rock gradually fell to the river on one side and grew again back up the plain on the other.

I beached my canoe at the base of a narrow, white-sandstone wall that towered four hundred feet above the river. Over the centuries, wind and rain bored a hole completely through the formation known, simply, as Hole in the Wall. Bodmer had painted this, too, and I decided as I entered the Upper Missouri National Wild and Scenic River that I would climb to the hole if I had the chance. The trail to the top of the cliff snaked through a sheep yard with a small hay hut and metal and plastic feeders. A truck road disappeared up the river bank.

Tromping through sage and scrub to the base of the long, vertical gray sandstone wall, I bullied my way up a cleft, climbing with my back against one side and my feet against the other. I slipped and scraped my arms and elbows. My hands were raw from scrabbling up away from Eagle Creek's canyon. They started to bleed again, leaving streaks on the rock. I imagined myself sliding down the cleft and lying on the bottom with a broken ankle or leg. But I wasn't going to fall, dammit. Then, suddenly, wide vistas opened over my shoulder. A few more struggling moves and I broke out on top of the wall, smacking dust from my shirt and breathing heavily.

I gasped. I'd seen photographs people had taken from this point above the river. But no picture captures a vista better than one's own eyes. I felt as if I stood below the roof of the world. The hazy sky drew down from cerulean blue to yellow white, where it melted into the hills. The top of the wall ran flat from the apex into the sagebrush plain. There, the white and beige sandstone grew into knobby, rounded outcrops and mushroom gardens.

I walked out to the precipice. Leaning into a stiff wind, I fought the urge to drop to my knees. The height and the outlook across the river made me feel powerful and good. I looked down and felt drawn into the space. The river arced like a smooth blue ribbon through its bottoms. Either side of the river, brown hills fluttered up to dry plains wrinkled and scarred with deep breaks and ravines. Standing there, battered by the wind, I felt calm. I sat down after a while and stared at the river until the sun fell toward evening. No one was out there but me.

For no good reason at all, I remembered how, after I'd sobered up, I felt like a scared grade-schooler when I wanted to do just about anything, from asking a woman to a movie to taking a new road home. I didn't really know how to be an adult or even what an adult was. I gazed into the distance and realized that I didn't know how to do any of this. I'd never been a father before and wasn't going to do it right all the time. I'd never been sober in a relationship with a woman, but maybe it was time to try. I thought again about how comfortable I'd felt with myself the last few days. Just admitting the wrongs of my past and trying to sort them out brought me closer to myself than I had ever come before, drunk or sober.

I left my perch only reluctantly. The Missouri sped my boat and me on toward the Judith River, where there was a BLM campground. On the way, the Missouri narrowed between steep banks and grew innumerable rows of standing waves. The white sandstone and the volcanic dikes gave way to bluffs of red and brown. What white sandstone remained now was laced with swatches of gray, brown, and black that matched the layers in the bluffs beyond.

I pulled into Judith Landing and staked out a campsite in a grove of stumpy, twisted cottonwoods. Once ashore, I boiled water for coffee on my pack stove. This had become a ritual upon landing my boat at the end of the day. When the water began to boil, I turned down the flame and poured the grounds in the water. A burst of foam sprung up and after a moment collapsed on itself, releasing that aroma that turns bad moods into good, and good moods into better ones.

I sat drinking strong, sweet coffee at a picnic table under a big cotton-wood. The Judith River, small enough to be a creek, joined the Missouri just in front of me.

"Cowboy coffee," said a man behind me. Larry Haight, a BLM volunteer who ran the campground at the landing, introduced himself.

"It's the best coffee, really," he said. "I have a coffeemaker over there in the trailer." With a thumb over his shoulder, he indicated a big RV at the back of the campground. "I never use it though. I'd rather have it your way."

"Join me? There's room," I said, looking at the picnic table.

"You bet."

"Sit down?" I said.

"If that's what it takes."

Having someone around felt good after a few days and nights alone. Larry was friendly and pleasant, but I would have welcomed just about any but the meanest company. He told me he was a retired letter carrier who volunteered every summer as campground host for the BLM at Judith Landing. I got the feeling he did it for his health. He had broad shoulders, hair going white, and deep-set blue eyes. He looked to be in his late forties. His legs were strong, and he wore sensible boots. His ruddy complexion had the well-tanned look of someone who spent time on the water. He asked if I fished and told me the way to his best fishing hole.

I rigged some line with a small hook and weight and canoed up the Judith to the place Larry had described. In no time, I pulled in a couple of flathead catfish on a piece of summer sausage. My thoughts got lost in the sun reflecting off the water. I felt sleepy and decided to quit pestering wildlife, since I didn't mean it harm anyway. I lay back and felt the boat rock while I watched the tree branches in the breeze. Night passed without a whisper.

Larry came into my camp with the sun. We talked for a long time over coffee. He brought out maps and atlases. He handled them with a kind of reverence.

"I'm from Nebraska," he said, "A town just south of Lincoln." He traced his index finger over a state highway map. "It sounds to me you went along this road."

He talked of towns along my path to Helena: Beatrice, Friend, North Platte, Kimball, and Gering. I told him about the people I had met in those places and details of my trip. He recognized stretches of road by my descriptions and asked me questions that revealed how well he knew the area. After we had talked our way across the map of Nebraska, he pulled out a gazetteer of Wyoming and then topographical maps of Yellowstone.

"I can look at maps for hours," he said. "The town names, the roads, the colors. All of them mean something, something important. And maps are good long after the roads have changed. You see, you can go back through maps of a place, all the different updates and versions. You see the changes in those places. They tell us where we've been, how far we went, and what we still need to see."

Larry took me twelve miles up a gravel road to a ranch. The rancher was kind enough to let me use the phone in his machine shed. Inside the shed was a jumble of farm implements, lathes, grinders, every sort of small engine, and a few large ones. But nowhere was there the dust of disuse. The rancher—a leathery, friendly man in greasy jeans and work boots—used nearly everything in the shed at different times of the year to tend his huge spread.

The phone was an old dial model on a wall. It was yellow somewhere under years of grease. I dialed my daughter. The place was so remote an operator had to place my call. As I waited, the days away from home and the length of the trip still to travel felt heavy. When she answered, homesickness I didn't realize I had welled up in sobs. I tried to control myself but couldn't. Fat tears fell in spatters on the concrete floor. I have rarely in my life cried like that.

Then I thought of myself, in rough-and-tough country, in the middle of the Montana plains, above a remote stretch of river, crying—in a pole barn, surrounded by worn tools and parts, augers and fence-post drivers, spilled oil and rusty machinery. I laughed until I cried again.

"Are you crying?" Sydney asked. "Why are you crying? Everything's all right."

"Yes, honey, I know," I said. "I'm just glad to hear your voice. I'm sorry I sound so crazy."

"No," Sydney said. "You don't sound crazy. You're my daddy. When are you coming home?"

She was just a four-year-old kid. What was I doing wandering around the landscape when I should be home raising her? I didn't want to scare her with big, heaving sobs. I made an excuse and got off the phone after only a few minutes and cried some more.

Larry waited patiently outside in the truck, watching the sagebrush whip in the wind. He was quiet as we bumped back toward the campground over the dirt track.

"Tough, isn't it?" he said after a time.

"Yeah, I lost it back there," I said. "Really boo-hooed up the place."

"First time in a while, wasn't it?"

"The last time I cried like that was in Topeka, Kansas," I said. "I talked to my kid there on a pay phone almost four months ago. It was cold. My feet hurt. She was eating ice cream."

"Crying like that felt better this time, didn't it?" he said.

"Yeah."

Larry, I think, understood being alone in the landscape for a long time. The sound of a human voice, the touch of a hand connects with something deep and special, a need for human contact. A familiar voice goes right into the heart. I looked over at him. He drove with one hand draped over the steering wheel. He was right. It did feel better than before. Sydney's voice tapped into a love and caring that was fundamentally me. It felt good.

I was still recovering from my emotional jag when Larry and I carried my canoe and gear over to the public boat ramp at the campground. I was sorry to have to tell him goodbye. But it was time to go home. I was still a month or more away from Kansas City, but I didn't regret the distance. Being away was good for me, and I knew I would be home soon enough. In the meantime, I wanted every minute of every day.

When the canoe broke free from land, I felt like I was flying. My thoughts became one with the river, and I recalled with a smile my crying in the machine shed. Homesickness is a funny thing. I've seen people go home a day after they left or after weeks and months, just as they were about to arrive at their destinations. Homesickness never bothered me much. It's an affliction that comes in spells, with the memory of a loved one or an ache for a familiar comfort. I always wanted someone or something to hold me accountable and relieve me of responsibility for my actions and their consequences. I wanted absolution for my original sin—the sin of being me. But I had to hold myself accountable. The law might come after me if I quit paying child support or abandoned my child. Punishment was no reason to live up to my responsibilities, stay sober, and be a decent father. Doing right by my own soul was far more important. I would go to work because I wanted safety and security for my daughter and me. I'd do it because I believed my daughter mattered.

Lost in these thoughts, I paddled steadily and easily all day. The Missouri squirreled around coulees and breaks that became deeper, more jagged, and more frequent. The river entered a long narrow canyon where isolated bottoms spread dark green into narrow defiles of red-brown and gray sandstone. Eroded cracks in the bluffs twisted into vast badlands of jagged spires. Rapids named Gallatin, Dauphin, Castle Bluff, and Bird once stopped steamboats or wrecked them in low water. With the river running high now, these same obstacles ruffled the water but barely rocked my boat. There was not a tree in sight. Some thirty-eight miles after I left Judith Landing, I ran the boat aground on a lonely spit of land, a former sandbar that a few cottonwoods had made their own. I realized as I stepped to shore that I hadn't said a word out loud all day.

On the opposite side of the river, Cow Creek flowed into the Missouri through a broad gash in the plains above. Grass and sagebrush led up to jagged sandstone bluffs layered in pale yellow, brown, and gray. Under a clear sky, the windless air left the river glass smooth, except for small swells and fish splashes. The sand near the cottonwoods was dry and soft. Only crickets broke the quiet. Geese and pelicans flew just inches above water. The sunset turned the river lavender and pink and then purple. In the middle of it all, I felt small and insignificant. Nothing I could say or shout would change that.

But it wasn't just landscape that grabbed hold of me. At the mouth of Cow Creek in the 1860s and 1870s, steamboat crews offloaded freight bound for Fort Benton. It wasn't an easy business. Since the Missouri above here was often impassable, wagoneers drove ox teams up the narrow confines of Cow Creek Coulee and out onto the upland prairies. Cow Creek itself winds like a cornered snake through its ravine. Freighters forded the creek dozens of times in the fifteen miles they traveled up onto the plains. The creek often ran in a trickle, at best, in the summertime. But a thunderstorm up the drainage meant flash floods, which often washed wagons, their drivers, and oxen into the Missouri.

Chief Joseph led almost seven hundred Nez Perce up Cow Creek Coulee after a short skirmish with federal troops and civilians at the landing on September 23, 1877. At the start of the day, the Nez Perce asked the small force of federal soldiers stationed at the landing for supplies. Fifty tons of goods-in-trade lay stockpiled at the landing. Private property—which the soldiers were there to protect—trumped the Native Americans' needs. The officer in charge gave the Nez Perce a few bits of hardtack and sent them on their way. Impatient warriors rode back to the landing in the evening, intent on demanding food for their starving people. After a long gunfight, the Nez Perce took what they needed and headed farther up the coulee. The U.S. Army had chased the Nez Perce for three months and over 1,200 miles through the Oregon, Washington, Idaho, and Montana Rockies. The Nez Perce mounted a military force of just two hundred warriors against thousands of federal troops. Women, children, and the elderly were starving and dying of illness. Joseph had a choice, and he chose the best of bad alternatives. The Nez Perce surrendered just eighty miles from the Canadian border.

Heat rising from the fire fluttered the leaves above. I couldn't imagine guiding seven hundred people anywhere—much less people ill-equipped for the journey, many of whom were old, hungry, and sick. I was only now learning my own way.

Even today, I'm not sure I navigate life well. As I stand in front of a college classroom, teaching history, I often wonder how I got there. Dumb luck? Probably. I don't really know what a career is. I've never had a clear vision for my future. When asked the question, "Where do you see yourself in five years?" I think, "Alive." On a construction job in the summertime, younger ironworkers look to me for guidance. Most of the time, I ignore the doubting voice in my head and fake it, hoping that I don't harm anyone with the allegedly wise and knowledgeable words I conjure from who knows where. If those students and ironworkers only knew how frightened I am . . .

After dark a beaver slid down the bank and into the water with barely a gurgle. It slapped its tail on the river and sent loud cracks into the veil of stars above. Finally, it realized, I suppose, I wasn't going anywhere. Silence settled again over the river as it eventually drifts over all things human, good and bad, joyful and terrible. Horrific things occurred along this river. Many more would again. People were here and gone. Chief Joseph. The army. All those bullwhackers and freighters. The steam-boat crews. The murderers, gamblers, thieves, and givers of solace and comfort. The river kept flowing.

I rested back on the ground. The chill of night crept in slowly, and my fire dimmed against the leaves of the tree. Beyond, the Great Swan flew along the Milky Way.

I don't know or care much if human beings have the eternal souls priests and nuns taught me about in Catholic school. But if they do, the spirits of the dead come to a place like the Missouri at Cow Creek. If not, then a place as serene.

9   Cheap Cigars

I HAVE TO GET USED TO SOLITUDE. WITHOUT THE DIN OF radios, televisions, and traffic, I discover again how much sound affects me. It distracts me, gnaws at the edge of my thoughts, and keeps me from looking inside too deeply. Televisions, radios, various kinds of music act on me like shiny things on kids and raccoons. Traffic divides my attention. When the sights and sounds of everyday life are not there, I seek them out, as if I have become comfortable only when distracted. In the absence of electronic noise; the sights of city life; and the sounds of traffic, air conditioners, and machines—long unspoken and often unrealized thoughts worm their way into my consciousness. In solitude I experience long bouts of perplexing doubt and, often, regret over slights large and small. Slowly these contemplations wash through, cleaning out my head as a flood flushes out a river. Solitude grows on me, and I learn to like being alone.

As much as the river befriended me and I was learning its languages, I needed human beings every now and then. Without them, I had nothing to soften the harder edges of my personality. My thoughts chased their tails in smaller, tighter spirals. A kind of emotional fragility set in, and I sometimes became irrational and unstable. I talked to myself and then went whole days without speaking a word or uttering a sound. Tiny frustrations escalated into angry fits, such as my letter-writing episode. When wind hindered my progress, I launched into strings of withering vulgarity. Time grew long or too short or both, depending on how my mind worked and whether I entertained or occupied myself well or not. The river possessed a rough, transcendent beauty when I remembered good times with girlfriends, places I had been with my daughter, or times when life had been easy. When I was down, I turned into a self-pitying grouch. The river became ugly, its demeanor human, mean, and personal. After cursing myself all morning, I broke into long fits of laughter at how small and self-occupied I'd been. Then I realized again that not everyone puts a boat on a river and floats away. Few people ever want to.

After Cow Creek the land changed and the bottoms grew wider. The rocky bluffs fell into rounder and gentler foothills. Stunted pines grew at the fringes of narrow bushy flats. These small trees gave way to forests of short and then graceful, tall pines and cedars. The fierce winds common in this region wrought less damage on the brittle cottonwoods and groves now stretched miles without break. The river soon spread out over a third of a mile. Dark shelves of mud and sand rambled out into the river below the bank. Wind took hold of the water, making it choppy and rough. But the spray rising off the waves relieved me from the heat.

I pulled the boat up to a ramp at a public river access. Walking up the ramp, I expected to find a park but never had a chance. As soon as I left the canoe, small painful pricks peppered my calves. "Neeah!" I shouted. I swatted what I thought were a few pesky mosquitoes. Then, as if on cue, the creatures descended on me in menacing clouds, whining like UFOs in 1950s science-fiction movies. At first, they landed painful bites on exposed flesh. Then they burrowed through my socks and shorts. My shirt provided no protection. I ran to the boat, dove in, and pulled on the paddle with all my strength.

A few of those mosquitoes, I swear, followed me the next twenty miles into the Charles M. Russell National Wildlife Refuge, a vast remnant of short-grass prairie named after the cowboy artist from Missouri. Fort Peck Lake ran through the middle of the refuge. The Army Corps of Engineers started the reservoir project in 1933, in part due to the Depression, in part due to the corps' ongoing expansion of its duties and power. They transformed 134 miles of river into a million acres of lake. I couldn't imagine the vastness of it all. The clouds of mosquitoes at that lake were even worse.

At the Kipp Recreation Area, whose boat ramp slid out into the lake under the Malta Bridge, I sloshed and slid around in deep, smelly mud. I hefted my dry bags and lifted the canoe up over my head, resting the center thwart across my neck and shoulders. My knees buckled. The heat fell on me like sandbags, and I broke into a soaking sweat. Swift movement kept mosquitoes from getting too much blood, but they made my run for higher ground a skip-and-dance. The canoe bounced, the bags slapped my butt and legs, and my shoes flopped up in my face. After dropping the canoe three hundred yards from the river, I slathered myself with repellent and wiped the mud from my face. At that moment, I thought myself rather grand. But in five minutes the mosquitoes attacked. Chemicals didn't stop them. I couldn't slap enough of them dead to make a difference. In Missouri the mosquitoes don't hurt much. But here they stung, and the stings pricked me from head to toe. In desperation I pulled on a nylon rain jacket against them. They bit right through it.

Then biting flies commenced their labors.

I built a fire thinking the smoke would ease the onslaught. Brushing and smacking, I set my tent, stowed my gear, and set some sticks alight. But it didn't help. All that smacking only attracted more flies and mosquitoes.

I wanted to call my daughter, and there was a phone at the other end of the rec area, about a third of a mile away under a beautiful and dark canopy of trees. Before I dove into the tent for the evening, I pulled the sleeves of the rain jacket down over my hands and the hood up over my head. I took off like a sprinter toward the phone. A minute of reprieve, I thought, was all I needed. Just a minute.

Near the phone was a boat and trailer belonging to two U.S. Fish and Wildlife Service volunteers. The men both looked exhausted. Thick clouds of mosquitoes hung over them, too, but they used the strategy of the old fox in Aesop's fable. When asked why the fox didn't shoo the thick layer of mosquitoes from his mangy hide, he said that the mosquitoes had eaten their fill. To swat the sated pests only made room for new, hungry ones.

I tried that while I talked to my daughter, but I wasn't used to the pain yet. Instead, I flapped my arms and danced around, sputtering, blowing mosquitoes out of my mouth and nose.

On my way back to my tent, I passed an old man and woman with a minivan parked in the dim light under the cottonwoods. They chased each other around their car in circles, cursing each other and the insects.

Under the trees, they set cans of household insecticide that laid in a low fog around the van. As far as I could see, it affected the evil, whining clouds not at all. The woman sprayed household bug killer on the old man, who wore a shirt already sodden with sweat and insecticide.

"This will take care of 'em," the woman said. But nothing stopped those mosquitoes. The man groaned, slapped his legs, and took off running again.

Just getting into my tent was slaughter. I unzipped the fly enough to squeeze in and still admitted thousands of the pests. I spent ten minutes wiping whole populations of mosquitoes into bloody streaks on the nylon canvas. Then, despite my fatigue, the incessant high-pitched whine of thousands of tiny wings kept me awake. They were out there, waiting. All I had to do was let down my guard.

The next morning, I was glad to be underway. The boat moved at a clip that kept the breeze fresh and the mosquitoes and flies from chasing me down. I washed the blood out of my shirt in the river and rinsed myself off with a bailer I'd made from a two-liter pop bottle.

Within a few miles the river slowed as it entered Fort Peck Lake. The work paddling felt good. The breeze kept the bugs at bay. I made good time and soon was ten miles into the lake. The water still flowed and helped along. Long stands of trees, now lapped in several feet of water, marked the river channel. The current drew small ripples and waves against the willows, which grew to heights of five and six feet. A tall bluff closed in on one side, and a bank of willows grew wider on the other. The floodplain, most of which was under water, rose up into pine- and cedar-topped hills.

Suddenly, the river disappeared, and I became lost in a labyrinth of willow trees. The bluffs receded into the distance, and I couldn't keep track of my direction. The overcast sky provided no help. The compass was useless, as I didn't know which way I was supposed to go. I moved in circles, I thought, because I'd seen these willows or those before. Clear spaces in the trees became dead ends.

After a while, the absurdity of my predicament overcame my worry. John Neihardt, I remembered from *The River and I*, experienced everything I'd encountered and suffered mostly his own complaints. My favorite travel writer, Eddy Harris, wrote in his river book, *Mississippi Solo*, how he also met bad weather and cranky wildlife. People shot at him. Motorboats almost ran over me. I got 'et by mosquitoes. Well-meaning Jet Skiers nearly swamped my boat. All that was a hell of a lot different than someone shooting at me.

Or being lost in the bushes.

These men endured, as had the countless Native Americans, fur traders, river men and women, and settlers who used this river. I could get by. I possessed no talents but perseverance and hard work, and I took faith in that. I picked a direction and paddled. The sky cleared and turned the water between the willows from shades of blue to black. I chased down the occasional splash or swish in the water, saw that the willow clusters sometimes formed spacious rooms, and noticed the kinds of spiders and insects that made the willows their homes. The mosquitoes weren't so bad here, and, I hoped, I had passed the worst of them.

Slowly, imperceptibly at first, the willows grew shorter and shorter. Through the afternoon and into early evening the spaces between them expanded, and the lake became wider. Finally, the willows sank beneath the surface of the water and disappeared, revealing a long, narrow lake between high, rounded sagebrush hills.

I chose a spit of land with piles of driftwood and set camp. The lake was as smooth as a mirror. No current rippled its surface. I landed the boat, gathered up armfuls of wood, and looked forward to a big fire.

Sitting down next to the fire, this time under a hum of a few hundred mosquitoes instead of a few million, I went over my map. I paddled some forty miles that day, at least twenty-five of them in the lake, for a total of over three hundred since I put in at Wolf Creek. I'd had difficulties. Storms. Heat. Insects. I'd heard of ten-foot waves and punishing winds on the lake but had encountered none. I believed I'd experienced all my river horrors.

I got comfortable next to the fire. A dinner of black beans, polenta, and strong coffee settled in, and I felt content. I drained away the last bit of coffee and listened to the startling silence. The cigar I fished out of one of my dry bags was excellent beyond its cheap-cigar price.

Then the end of the cigar popped, and ash dropped onto my shirt.

I thought it was funny. My cigars were cheap for just this reason—to entertain me sometimes. Then the fire snapped, and a bit of wood whizzed by my ear in a little singing whistle. Soon, the fire erupted in plumes of snaps and sparks. The burning wood popped me in the forehead and on the legs and burned little holes in my shirt. The grass near the fire smoldered in a hundred spirals of rising smoke. I cursed and danced around stomping out burning embers. I grabbed sparky logs from the fire by their unburned ends and heaved them into the river. I stomped out one tiny wisp of smoke and ran to another, in a hurried circle around the fire. When I'd tramped out all the sparks, I poured the water in my bottles into the fire's smoldering remains.

I picked up a log from the mountain of driftwood nearby. Years and miles in the water wore away the bark and rounded the ends. I whittled a little sliver from the gray surface of the log. Red cedar! Oak and pine crackle and sputter. But cedar snaps and flings little pieces of hot shrapnel. I learned about cedar the first time I threw it in a fire as a young Boy Scout on an overnight. That time, I caused a panic among my compatriots when the wood started snapping and people started running.

Sitting on the bank, I looked up into the dried grass and piney woods beyond. Cedar studded the hills upstream for many miles, which accounted for it among the driftwood. The thought of the potential consequences of my negligence and hurry to have fire gave me a chill. What would a guy do when he started a forest fire so far from the road? Just push the canoe into the water and move on? Hope nobody would find him out?

For the first time since I put in at Wolf Creek, I did without fire and, instead, watched the river until long after sunset.

By midmorning the next day, I'd canoed only five miles before heavy wind ground my journey to a stop on a flat, mushy sandbar. The lake widened to almost two miles. Hot blasts hammered my hastily pitched tent. Between gusts, mosquitoes formed thick, smokelike billows over my shelter, but sweltering heat inside kept them out. I laid in the tent as long as I could and then walked around in circles outside. The side of my body to the wind harbored no bugs at all, but they covered the other like brown fur. I went back into the tent. Sweat from my fingers soaked book pages and smeared ink in my journal. I listened to waves crack in a small tubelike depression under the cap of grass along the shore. When I could no longer stand the heat and the pacing, I hiked up into the grassy hills that rose from the lake.

But then I figured I wouldn't get anywhere if I didn't try, so I struck the tent and paddled for hours close to shore, making just two hundred yards in murderous wind and four- and five-foot swells. The gray, featureless sky sat low on the landscape and broke into rain. After a time, I took to the water once more and made only about 150 yards before pulling the boat out of the swells. I donned my rain gear against the mosquitoes but soon took it off because of the heat, a process I repeated over and over again — mosquitoes, rain gear, heat and sweat, no rain gear, quick relief from the heat, then mosquitoes. There was little to do but lean into the wind and watch the water.

But I couldn't just watch. I'm not good at just sitting, though I wish I were. That day, I'd already read, napped, and written as much as I could stand. I needed movement or at least the feel of it. I put the boat in and bobbed in the waves around spits of land jutting into the lake. I paddled up swells topped with spray and then paddled down the other side. After an hour and two hundred or so yards, a five-foot wave set the canoe ashore with a jolt. I pulled the boat away from the water, sat down on a log, and started putting on and taking off the rain gear again.

Between one of these gyrations, a dull, deep pain shot up and across my back and up into hair. My pants caught fire. "Shit. Goddamn. Godfuckingdammit. Sonnuvabitch." I flung my shorts and undies, boots and socks into the sagebrush. I smacked and brushed tiny red ants from my arms and legs. I picked them out of my ears and from between my toes. Naked and rotating in the wind to move the mosquitoes around, I finally jumped into the cold water and sloshed around in the mustard-brown waves with logs and sticks and all kinds of organic debris. My feet stirred up clouds of stinky, black mud. The waves knocked me under the water. Sputtering, I climbed out, angry and frustrated but oddly refreshed.

Dressed again in ant-free clothes, I pitched the tent on a grassy shelf above the lake and tied the canoe to some scrub in a ravine below. I dove out of a mosquito cloud into the tent. Killing all the mosquitoes inside took twenty minutes and left red hairy meteor streaks across the nylon. The day turned dim as night. The sound of wind across the water and the breaks became indistinguishable from the crashing of the waves.

After a while, I couldn't stay in the tent and walked up to the plain above. Lightning cracked the darkness and illuminated cedar- and pine-topped hills in the distance. Plumes of insect repellent flew mostly into the wind. A pack of coyotes ran up out of the brush in a ravine and across the bumpy plain. A herd of mule deer and a red fox fled in the opposite direction and took refuge from the wind in the brushy breaks. Hawks soared off the plain and then high up over the lake.

The sky, already a deep green gray, darkened further. The wind grew stronger. The smell of rain erupted among the odors of sagebrush and lake water. Waves on the lake transformed into white haystacks. Gusts broke across the far shore about a mile and a half away and raced across the lake — the air visible in lines of gray mist. The winds broke ashore and flattened grass in arcs that swept up past me. Swirls of spray, similar to dust devils on the prairie, danced over the water. I walked farther up the rise. The sky grew darker and the landscape became luminous with lightning flashes. A twister started down from the clouds, thrashing like a bullwhip. A spiral of spray rose on the far shore below it and twisted up into the low clouds. The white waves' tops drew up and into it like tentacles. The spout zigzagged toward my shore. And then, as quickly as it formed, it disappeared, leaving white coils of steam racing across the lake.

My hair stood on end. I raised my hands and face into the wind and felt electricity race through me. The wind again increased, and I leaned into it, taking delight in the power of the storm. I don't know how long I stood there, pushing against the wind, yelling and screaming. Suddenly, something instinctive told me the fun was over. I dove into the tent at the instant a lightning bolt hit the hill above. Thunder shook the ground and compressed the sides of the tent, which the wind jerked back and forth. Gusts bowed the nylon down against my back. Only the weight of my body kept the tent on the ground. The thunderclaps left loud ringing in my ears, over which I could hear nothing. Through the canvas on my back, I felt the rain begin, then hail. Lightning repeatedly struck the hill above and the trees in the ravines close by. As my hearing returned, the wind sounded like airliners flying low overhead.

And I was overjoyed. I laughed and bellowed. I cheered the storm along. I don't know where the mirth came from, but I had no fear. Nothing in my being felt threatened. I yawped and yelled and screamed and screeched.

The storm blew for hours, never decreasing in strength. Then, long after nightfall and within just a minute, the wind faded into a gentle breeze. The downpour turned into steady, easy rain for a short while and then stopped. I climbed out of the tent and watched the lake, which had settled quickly and reflected the stars. Sitting on my rain jacket next to the tent, I stared at the lake until I nodded off with my head on my knees.

In the night, the wind died completely, and mosquitoes bit me awake. As I settled into the tent and spread red mosquito droplets against the canvas, I thought of my situation. I had food. Water, while murky and in need of settling and treatment, was near. My meager equipment was holding up. I'd felt loneliness but nothing serious. Patience and tolerance for myself and nature were in short supply. But they would be back, I figured, after some sleep and a few miles of good paddling.

I could feel the river under the lake somewhere.

10   Oaths and Vulgarities

AFTER A WHILE, TWENTY MILES A DAY ON FLOWING RIVER was just jacking around. Most days, I canoed thirty to thirty-five miles. When I entered the lake, I resolved to continue this. It might mean more effort, more time in the boat, but I'd also get across the behemoth Fort Peck Lake in days rather than weeks.

Most of the time, I plan to fail. That way I deflect blame from myself for botching what I set out to do. But sometimes I fool myself into believing my delusions will come true. Self-deception softens the jagged boundaries of fear. I get over myself and get started.

But nothing ever matches the dreams of success I build in my head. After almost setting the forest aflame, I paddled just ten miles in four days, nine of those miles to where I'd witnessed the storm. Over the following three days, I fought fierce wind for every yard, every foot of that last mile. At the end of the third day, I walked back to where I had camped in the storm for a knife I'd left behind. The walk through ravines and along the shore took me less than a half an hour. In the end, I might have made better time if I'd put the boat on my shoulders and walked.

Now the river took me where I didn't want to go. Putting my boat on the water at night when the air was still and the lake was smooth terrified me. In the darkness, the river still reared up at me like the fanged creature in the closet of my youth. At the same time, I needed miles behind me for my own mental health. Making no progress made me angry. I was in a constantly foul, cursing mood. I'd come up out of those emotional depths to laugh at the absurdity of my situation, only to sink again into deep, brooding depression.

So here I went. Though brutal during the day, the wind died after sunset and didn't start again until well after dawn. I decided that I'd paddle as far as I could before the sun came up and, if I had to, stop during the day. At the very worst, I reasoned, I'd lose the boat to the lake and hike through miles of prairie to civilization. That was uncomfortable. But standing around in the mosquitoes made me plenty miserable already.

Doing something is always better than doing nothing. I woke early, broke camp quickly, and was out on the water before I had the chance to talk myself out of it. Dawn added deep purple to the starry darkness. Paddling worked the sleepiness out of my head, and I felt good and refreshed. In the dim light of dawn, I was no longer a frustrated, fearful man. I watched the shore glide by. Mule deer and coyote looked up and stared awhile before bolting up the ravines and over the rises. The air smelled of sagebrush and cedar. I found I could travel better than I had imagined. The land transformed from silver to dark gray to shades of brown spotted with green. The water was smooth. I could only hear my breath and the rhythmic thump of the paddle and the slosh of water against the boat.

Before I knew it, sunrise burst on the water in orange and red. I had gone about ten miles and made a good many more before the air began to stir. But once the sun was up, the water began its rise and fall in long, even swells. An hour after sunup, the gentle breeze whipped into a ferocious blast. Swells now broke over the bow. The waves pulled the boat away from shore and into open water no matter how hard I paddled. After twenty miles, the waves peaked in white foam, and I made no headway at all. I pulled into a small cove. Clouds of mosquitoes settled on me as I stepped ashore.

I pitched the tent in a small depression and set the door into the hot wind bullying up through the coarse, dry grass. Despite the wind, the tent soon grew too hot for me. I tossed and turned. Sweat soaked my self-inflating mattress. From time to time, I suffered the mosquitoes and took walks along an old road that brush and grass reclaimed for the prairie.

By late afternoon I again felt lonely and anxious. My map indicated that the Crooked Creek Recreation Area lay four miles up the jagged shoreline and across a mile of open water—lake I'd have to traverse without a bank or shore for refuge. The map showed that the rec area opened only seasonally. I hoped I came at the right time of year and that someone was there now. I hung on the chance of seeing a human being after a week alone. I struck the tent and set the canoe to water. Human company after not seeing anyone but people spraying each other with insecticide . . . I was determined to make it down the shoreline and across the open water if it killed me.

For the next three and a half hours, waves crashed over the bow and into the boat. I made slow but steady progress. I struggled to stay close to shore and out of the wind. Then I rounded a spit of land pushed into the open water. The wind blew without hindrance. Waves turned into five- and six-foot canoe swallowers. I cursed the holy name of Franklin Delano Roosevelt, whose administration built this lake. I cursed the Corps of Engineers and all those men and women who dammed the river. Uttering oaths and vulgarities, I wrenched the canoe up the side of a swell and then paddled down the other to avoid being blown backward. The canoe settled at the bottom of troughs, and I pulled hard to keep it perpendicular to the waves. After a while, I could see the campground on the other shore when the canoe lurched up again over the walls of water.

The Missouri may be my friend, I thought, but shitfire . . .

I was angry, not frightened or terrified. The canoe pulled one way and then the other. Waves and wind tried to capsize it. My back, stomach, and arm muscles burned and cramped. Halfway across the lake arm, the wind caught the canoe and spun us on top of a wave. I paddled in response but was not fast or strong enough. I felt the boat going over until the next wave caught it and pushed us upright again. The canoe rode sideways up the swells and between walls of translucent milky-green water. The wind whirled it perpendicular to the waves again. Like a big surfboard, it rode waves until they raced ahead. I paddled as quickly and deeply as I could. At the top of each wave the campground drew just a little bit closer. Finally, a breaker settled me and my boat on shore at the campground.

I stood from the boat, but the world reeled beneath me, as if I were trying to stand on a trampoline that people kept jumping on. I fell flat on the ground. I stood and stumbled forward in lurching steps. Falling again, I stayed on my hands and knees, looking at the rocky ground. My head spun. It reminded me of being drunk, and I laughed. The rocky ground where I kneeled sloped up from the lake into steep, rocky hills draped in scrubby cedar. The arm of the lake I'd crossed disappeared into a grove of cottonwoods at the base of the hills several miles away. The waves coming out of the lake arm looked like a diagram of sound waves from a horn.

As far as I knew, the rec area was one of those ghost-town places in the West, where everyone just picked up and left. It resembled the knots of prospectors' cabins and sheep herders' shacks that I found hiking in the Wyoming Rockies. Except for the patinas of rust on the hinges and antiquated food tins in the cabinets, they looked as if someone had walked out of them the day before. Here empty numbered campsites branched off a dirt track through the brush. Beyond the campground, sagebrush and bunch grass grew up between dusty boats and travel trailers parked in a fenced storage area. A small wooden building, the camp store, stood under the rocky hills where the road came down to the lake. When I could stand, I stretched and walked slowly around the place. The only sign of life was a truck with an empty boat trailer near a concrete boat ramp. I stumbled like a drunk up to the camp store and peeked in the windows. The door was locked. Inside was dark.

People or no people, I was not paddling one yard farther in that lake. I wandered around the campground and down to the boat ramp, deciding where to pitch my tent. But I didn't do much other than look out over the lake. The adrenalin faded, and my vision became clearer. I entered that state where I just don't care one way or another about much at all.

As I waded into the water at the end of the boat ramp, a dog howled and barked. I looked over and saw a fifth-wheel trailer I hadn't noticed. A shirtless man in cutoffs came around the opposite side. He was buff and tanned. A small goatee and moustache graced his round face. He squinted. His eyeglasses turned darker in the sunlight. Next to him jogged an English bulldog with a spiked collar, bottom teeth jutting from its lip.

"How're you?" he said. "I didn't hear you drive up. Where's your car?"

"I don't have one. I surfed in on that." I pointed to the canoe, waves crashing on the shore around it.

"Yer shittin' me," he said. He stopped and raised his hand against the sun. "Good for you. That water looks like a bummer . . . Hey, I'm Kevin Scoby, and this here's Spike. You're lucky. Me and Spike was headed out to Winnett."

"Winnett?" I said.

"Yeah, the closest town to here," he said. "It's fifty-five miles away, and I want to be there by five, so we gotta get on the hump."

I looked at the store, which was about as big as a two-car garage. "You have a cola and a candy bar in there I could buy?"

"Yeah, I got something like that," he said.

After being in the wind all day, the store interior felt eerily still. It was a spare place. Except for some fishing tackle and insect repellent, shelves along the walls were mostly empty. I pulled a cola and a candy bar from a glass-fronted cooler. Kevin busied himself behind the counter, making notes on a small pad. I hadn't had money in my pocket for over two weeks.

"I have to run out to the canoe," I said. "My money's out there."

"It's on me." He looked out at the lake through a window next to the case. "I oughta give you a medal."

"Could I ride into town?" I asked. "I need a few things."

"Sure, buddy. I expected you'd go along, anyway."

In his small pickup, we ascended the rocky track out of the valley to the plain above and drove over a furrowed and washboarded dirt road. We sped across a vast plain of rolling hills covered with sagebrush and brown grass. Fences laced the landscape. Cows stood here and there. We saw only a few houses, mostly miles from the road.

Kevin told me he was from Michigan but wound up "on that rock" through an uncle who knew the leaseholder for the rec area.

"It's just a summer job, you know, but it's a good one," he said. "Everyone around comes down, mostly ranchers between the rec area and Winnett. They get away from their spreads on the weekends. During the week, I'm lucky to see anyone. That guy whose truck was down by the ramp went out on his boat on Monday. I ain't seen him since." It was Wednesday, which meant Kevin had also been alone the last couple of days.

"So, I'm lucky," he continued. "The last time I saw anybody in the middle of the week was some really crazy guys canoeing just like you. Their equipment looked pretty shabby, and they didn't hardly have enough stuff between them to do much good. They really looked bad, too. Grubby, you know, like they hadn't eaten enough or cleaned up at all. But they had lotsa weed with 'em, so I guess that made up for food and whatnot. They smoked more dope in the few days they were here than I seen some stoners smoke in a month."

The ride into town was a real teeth-chatterer. Kevin talked and gestured, sped and skidded. He fishtailed around corners and drove eighty miles an hour where the dirt track was straight. Over gully and washboard, he never slowed down. I white-knuckled it most of the way. But bouncing across prairies and over hills was exciting and fun. I was used to the world passing at canoe speed.

Swerving and jerking across the dry hills and into the sandstone breaks, Kevin babbled like a man who had been alone too long. His thoughts bounced around. He yelled most of the time and used his hands too actively. When he laughed, he brayed like a mule. He was twenty-four, vibrant, outgoing, and rugged. He loved his job. He said he liked talking up the campers and boaters — when any were around — keeping the place clean, and having plenty of time to himself. He knew he wouldn't be there forever and that this job was one of many he would have before he discovered what he wanted to do. As he went on and on, I was just glad to listen to him, to hear a human voice. It was all the easier because he was a likable guy who had no bad words for anyone.

Even so, I felt relieved when Kevin slid onto the graded dirt streets of Winnett. The town was an eight-block square in a small valley between grassy mesas. Home to 170 souls, it was the only town in Petroleum County, and it had seen better days. An oil boom in the 1940s had swelled the town's population to nearly two thousand. While oil was still the big business in Petroleum County, the town had now emptied. Automation in the oil fields eliminated many workers. Bigger and more efficient farm machinery as well as land, agriculture, and ranching consolidation scattered the rest. Houses and stores in town stood abandoned in that western sort of way — gray bowed wood, broken windows, and empty sagebrush lots. A lonely and idle grain elevator stood on the edge of town, the tallest building anywhere around. Billings, the only major city nearby, was ninety miles to the north. Lewistown, a farm town, lay seventy miles to the east. The entire population of all seventeen hundred square miles of Petroleum County was hardly five hundred people, making it one of the least populated counties in the continental United States.

Main Street was mostly empty, too, except for a bar and a couple of other businesses. At a hardware-grocery-convenience store, Kevin jawed up the owner, between picking things off shelves for the campground and for himself. I bought a few jars of peanut butter, some dried-noodle dinners in pouches, and mustard for my summer sausage. The owner of the store wandered around behind us, complaining about the federal government. He talked about how the feds were planning to take away his guns . . .

"And I got a plan to fight them off," he said. "Just like a lotta people around here — we ain't gonna stand for no more federal intrusion."

"Into what?" I said.

"Into everything. The IRS, EPA, FBI, OSHA, all them. They want it all. I won't have anyone tell me my business."

"But who maintains these roads here?" I asked. Kevin coughed and elbowed me in the ribs. He mouthed, "Shut up. Time to go."

"BLM, goddammit, and they better keep after it."

It was poisonous stuff, and I'd heard it all my life. The conservative Catholic family I grew up in favored the John Birch Society and antifeminist, pro-gun politics. My father frequented reactionary Catholic groups. Everywhere, communist conspiracies, one-world governments, and anti-Christian agendas of the Democratic Party and "liberals" sapped American energy and produced phalanxes of faceless collectivists. My dad got whipped up into an NRA, pro-gun catchphrase frenzy when he got to drinking, and he talked frequently about hiding his guns from the government. My family did not condone mistreatment of anyone. But some of them maintained that Martin Luther King Jr. sought communist help for the civil rights movement. He was, according to some, just "stirring up the Negroes" for his own reputation and benefit.

I aped this reactionary language and thinking well into my teens, when the profound confusion it produced in me became unbearable. What my family, friends, and priests told me matched little what I felt or experienced myself. When I read the newspaper and listened to the news, it didn't seem that socialists, feminists, and "pro-abortionists" meant to harm anyone. I had black friends in school but had to sneak around with them when we weren't in school for fear of getting caught. In Boy Scouts my mates made fun of gay people, but my gay friends didn't deserve it. They never violated me or my space, or anyone else's for that matter. Finally, when I was fifteen, I announced at a family gathering that if Christian morality and the American way were so good and right, it didn't make sense that some changes would do them irreparable harm. My father grew red in the face. "That's just what communists want you to think!" he yelled. I protested. My grandfather, my mom's father, wouldn't talk to me for almost a year.

I gained the chutzpah, in part, from deepening dependence on alcohol. The more I drank, the further that strange world of judgmental morality retreated from me. In the end, drinking and drugs released me from the injurious influences of my parents, flag-waving jingoists, persecuted Christians, and gun fetishists. And for that, I'm grateful.

God bless 'em all, I thought as I listened to the store owner. Everyone needs something to bitch about.

After we paid for our things, we drove over to the town pool hall, a dinky, dark room filled with high school kids who showed off to each other smoking cigarettes and cussing. ("Amateurs," I remember thinking. They still had learning to do.) Kevin and I shot pool. I felt my land legs returning after the lake and the wild drive. Later, at the municipal swimming pool, Kevin joshed around with the young men who seemed to have nothing to do. He talked a streak, hammed around for the girls, and posed for a kid taking snapshots, before we headed back to the lake.

We arrived back at camp past dusk. Kevin insisted I make a bed on a small couch in his trailer so I wouldn't have to worry about setting up camp and fighting mosquitoes in the dark. We talked for hours about home, girlfriends, and the outdoors. When, finally, our conversation died down, I settled into a comfortable place on the couch next to Spike, a dog that didn't smell like one. He snored all night.

I slipped out of the trailer long before Kevin or Spike woke. The day was still; the lake, like polished glass. I didn't look forward to getting back out there. Being alone was fine, but being stuck in the tent with nothing to do was awful. I could only read and write so much. Then I'd walk. I'd start away from the tent with the greatest of ambitions. Exploration! Discovery! Adventure! But after just a few miles, thick clouds of the insects drove me back. The tent was too hot for the mosquitoes, and I'd lie in there, sweltering. But a short time later, boredom and an anxious feeling that I might be stuck forever forced me to walk, starting the cycle over again.

Spike woke Kevin with a bark when I came back toward the trailer. Kevin set right to his work, and I helped. We tended to the campsites, evening out the gravel and picking up trash. We swept out the concrete pit toilets and then drove up out of the breaks to a small pond. Kevin pulled up minnow traps and dumped the shining, flipping fish into five gallon buckets to stock the tank at the store. We stopped by some buttes of white sandstone topped with strata of brown sandstone, gray shale, and coal, black as night. Rain and wind had eroded the sandstone into jagged spires and rounded mushrooms. Petrified wood lay about in chunks. Except for isolated bunches of razor grass that had found purchase where dust gathered in this badland, we might as well have been walking on the moon.

Kevin wanted to go to the Lewistown Fair that evening. Late in the afternoon, we made another wild drive that landed us in the café in the center of Winnett. The waiter was dignified and sure of himself as he put down silverware and glasses with overdramatic feminine motions. He possessed a mercurial sense of humor and flirted with Kevin and me between taking our orders and delivering heaping plates of food. I thought it nice that Kevin treated the waiter as his own friend and didn't get uptight or show any signs of discomfort being around him. It made me like Kevin all the more.

From our wanderings through town, I formed impressions of this small rural community. I'm sure there were good people in Winnett. But many of the boys and men I met were restless and bored. Outwardly friendly to me, many talked poorly of anyone and anything from outside the town and outside the norm. I couldn't divine whether they were opening up to me or trying to send me a message, or both. Some of the young men held deep resentment against townspeople who went to college and never came back. I had a feeling those same men didn't much relish palling around with college grads who came back either. In the short time I was with Kevin, I often heard from his acquaintances and others in town about "them brown people" overrunning Montana. I never saw any blacks or Hispanics in Winnett.

"Smartass easterners and city people don't fare well around here," one of the young men at the pool told me. He was ensconced in a deck chair and kept running his fingers around the hair on his chest.

"I'm from the city, and I'm a smartass," I said. I suspected he hadn't met many smartass inner-city types like me.

"Well, 'cept you, of course. You're different."

"No," I said. "I'm exactly like them."

"Aw, come on." He thought I had made a grand joke.

After dinner Kevin and I piled into a car with three of the other men from the pool and took off for Lewistown. Life in Petroleum County was much the same for these guys as for young men everywhere. They talked about sex, smoking dope, and drinking. They asked about where I lived. After I told them about my inner-city neighborhood, their questions revolved around race and ethnicity. Do you mind living around blacks? Were Mexicans lazy? I told them of the loyalty I felt toward my neighbors, friends, and coworkers, many of whom were immigrants and blacks and Hispanic Americans. In return, they all told me how relieved they were to get out of Winnett's crushing confines and what one of the boys called "closed-mindedness." To a man, they wanted to leave their hometown, find work, and build lives somewhere else. A melancholy quiet filled the car after a while. A thunderstorm flashed on the horizon, and we watched lightning spider across the treeless hills in the distance.

At the fair, the young men relaxed even more. We each took turns trying to beat the carneys in the midway games. Kevin and his friends roped me into riding a couple of the carnival rides, things that I generally avoid because they scare the daylights out of me. They laughed and enjoyed the flying, tumbling, and churning, while I gritted my teeth and scrunched my eyes closed. On the way back to Winnett, the lightning kept up. The thunderstorm was so close we could hear it, but it never struck.

"Man, you're quiet today," Kevin said the next morning as we drove down into the campground after spending the night in a small warehouse Kevin's boss owned in Winnett. It was Friday, and few trailers and boats stood on the gravel pads. We looked out over Crooked Creek and the Musselshell River. The wind had come back up, sending waves in crisscrossing patterns into the lake.

"There's another 650 miles of lakes after this one," I said. "That's tough to face now that I've tasted what it's like."

"Don't go out there today," he said. "When those stoners came through earlier this year, there wasn't a breeze for days. And they were two guys in a canoe. You're alone. You don't want to go out today. Look at it."

"Then tomorrow," I said. "I'll head out then."

"Are you kiddin'?" he said. "This is the windiest time of year. I'll take you to the Fort Peck Dam or Wolf Point on Tuesday, after the weekend traffic clears out of here. I got no one all week, and it would be fun."

"You're kiddin'," I said.

"My pleasure," he said.

I told him I'd think about it.

Later I drove into town to pick up ice for Kevin. About fifteen miles from the rec area, a man sitting on the blade of his bulldozer signaled me to stop. I stepped from the truck and introduced myself. He said he just wanted someone to have lunch with and wanted to know if I minded.

"I always bring extras just in case," he said and handed me a salami sandwich and a bag of chips. I thought it'd be nice to flag down strangers and feed them, just because it seemed like a great idea.

His name was Sandy, and he made a living moving earth around.

"Mostly, guys who go into excavation do a lot of different things," he said. "I do leveling. I either follow what an engineer and survey crew lay out for me to do, or I put out the stakes and strings myself. There's a special level I can put on the string. Then I push dirt around. That's all I do."

"But it must be more complicated than that," I said.

"Oh, sure," he said. "There's lots that goes into it; you gotta learn it. It takes practice. But the result is always the same, level dirt or a gravel pad." He poured himself steaming coffee from a metal thermos and crossed his legs. He leaned forward and rested an elbow on his knee, coffee in one hand, a cigarette in the other.

"You work by yourself all the time?" I said. The day was bright; and the land, stark and colorless. Intense midday sun washed away the color. It was quiet and absolutely gorgeous.

"Listen," he said. "I've been on road crews before and job sites with a hunnert guys. There could be a thousand guys. It don't matter. When that dozer starts up, with all the racket that diesel makes, you're always alone."

"So you just flag anyone down when it's time for lunch?"

"I thought you was Kevin," he said. "I live by myself out on a patch of rocks near Mosby, a town that don't even exist anymore. I camp out down there on Crooked Creek at the rec site. That's where I met him."

He grew serious.

"You know," he said, "I get awful lonely up there in my house. I useta be married, but the loneliness out here drove the woman off. Too bad for me. TV drives me crazy. I don't have much to do with those people in town. I'm from Winnett, grew up there. Even I don't think it's a nice place. Them people can be bastards.

"But I wouldn't give up my place up there at Mosby. Couldn't, not even for my wife. Most times it's nice. Quiet. Lotsa room for my mind to wander around. I don't think I'd take to livin' in a town, 'specially not Winnett, but any town, you know. Not anymore. Even here," he swept his hand over the horizon, "it ain't bad."

It was beautiful. A few cedars grew at the base of the grass-covered hills. In the ditch near where we sat, a stand of Russian olives swayed in the breeze.

On the way into Winnett and back, I thought about the lake, the complications of getting around it, and Kevin's offer of a ride. Before I made a decision, I called my uncle Phil in Kansas City from the phone at the campground store — I'd bought a prepaid phone card for occasions such as this and made collect calls most other times. Because it was a Friday, I knew he'd be at my grandparents' house for the evening. Philip and I had grown up together. He's the last of ten kids and only six months older than I am. For the last three decades, he had been my uncle, brother, and best friend. I wanted to go over what was in my mind with him and then call my daughter just to hear her voice.

Philip answered my grandparents' phone and told me his brother, my uncle Larry, had died. I had vertigo, the strange sensation that my world had stopped. I felt cold despite the heat.

Larry had been a troubled soul, in and out of institutions since his short tenure as a soldier in Vietnam. I had little to do with Larry the last years of his life but not because I didn't want to. He had been shut away, if not behind a locked door, then in his own troubled mind. Even so, his death shocked me.

The whole family on my mom's side was at my grandparents'. My parents flew in from Reno, Nevada, where they had moved from Kansas City in the early 1980s. My uncles Chris and Juan arrived that morning in Kansas City from their home in Monterrey, Mexico. Handing the phone to one another, everyone took turns talking to me. I tried to comfort them but couldn't help breaking up. They all encouraged me, even my grandfather. He told me that although I was insane and should be ashamed of myself for leaving a perfectly good four-year-old girl behind, I was doing something good.

After the call, I slumped down on the step of the store and cried. The wind had come up again, harder than before. White foam covered the lake. Larry was dead. I'd left my daughter for what was to be five months on this journey, giving the entire responsibility for her care to her mother. This trip seemed so selfish all of a sudden. What was I trying to prove?

I felt a million miles from home.

"Man, you don't have to look so down," Kevin said. He had a toilet brush and trash bag in his hands. "I ain't going to charge you even one dollar for being here."

I laughed. "There's no need for that," I said, wiping away the tears. "I have money with me."

"Yeah, but you did me a favor flopping out of that lake," he said. "You know what it's like to go all week with nothing to do and no one to talk to?"

"Yeah, kinda."

"So what," he said. "I'm lookin' forward to you saying yes to the ride."

"Yes, Kevin, you bet," I said. I wanted to be done with wind and the loneliness that came out of making so little progress. "I'll take a ride with you."

By telling Kevin, "Yes," I decided to travel the Missouri in a different way than I'd started out or expected to. I felt grief and a deep spasm of guilt for abandoning my initial plans. I told people I would canoe the Missouri all the way from Montana. What would they think? For over a year, I lived with the determination to make this journey a certain way, even ignoring or avoiding information that told me I couldn't or shouldn't make the trip at all. Was I letting myself down? Would that evening mark the start of a windless period that would let me paddle this lake without a problem? Was I trying to take the easy way home?

I sat there on the picnic bench and tried to answer those questions honestly to myself. Yes, I did care what people thought. It would matter to me if they thought less of me for not braving all the dangers and discomforts that came with a trip like this. But they weren't here. I wasn't letting myself down. I discovered what I was capable of and could stick out a journey until I was forced by health or dire circumstances to turn back. Sure, taking a ride with Kevin was easier than enduring the tedium of being hung up on the lake. But it was not the end of the journey. I wasn't just leaving my boat on the side of the lake and going home. This was turning into a different journey than the one I had planned. In the end, I liked the possibilities.

The last three days had been a good break. I'd spent time with an interesting man and learned some things about life in a forgotten, dusty corner of the American empire. I'd also sorted through some difficult things and made sound decisions accordingly. My mind made up, I felt a sense of peace.

That evening, several ranchers and their families sat by trailers in lawn chairs, drinking beer and grilling hamburgers. Vacationers from Colorado joined them at the campground. A happy couple from Saskatchewan pulled in with a funny little boat, a sort of half dory with a tiny cabin. They talked to each other in heavy Canadian accents. They were "involved in pharmaceuticals," they said.

"No kidding," I said. "I used to be involved in pharmaceuticals."

"Garsh, really?" the man said. "Who'd ya sell for?"

"Well, I was more of a buyer," I said with a wink.

"Oh, my," the woman said with a smile. "Before I met Devin here, I was involved in that kind of pharma, too. (wink, wink) Just for fun, you know."

"Oh, I know."

"Me, too," said the man, getting the gist of things. "Drugs made me just silly. I was a real downer kinda guy. Loved 'em. Got ahold of morphine more than once. Boy, oh, boy. Gave it up to sell it. There's a lot more money in it that way."

"People and their prescriptions, you know," the woman said. "We're gonna retire on 'em."

When a storm came up later in the evening, one of the campers' tents blew into the lake. The smiling Canadians loaded a drunken North Dakotan and a couple of ranchers in the funny boat and headed after the tent. It rolled ahead of them over white-topped swells. The North Dakotan hunkered down at the bow, yelling and flapping his arms. I could see him screaming, but the wind swallowed up whatever he was yelling. The harder the wind blew, the happier he looked and the faster the Canadians and their boat went to make it over the steep waves. Somehow they avoided pitching over backward. Soon they sped out into open water, facing the wind's full force. The boat disappeared over one swell and reappeared on top of the next. The North Dakotan held fast at the front of the ship.

People gathered in groups around the campground to watch. I ran with Kevin through heavy rain from one campsite to another. A group of men sat under a swaying awning on one of the RVs, drinking beer and smoking cigarettes. "Stupid fuckers," one said. "Those assholes shouldn't get their tent back," said another. "They were dumb enough not to stake it down," said the third. "Fuck 'em. That boat goes down, those idiots deserve it." They jeered like men who needed to impress one another. I figured they were from Winnett.

Finally the crowd on the boat retrieved the tent and spent another tedious twenty minutes fighting the wind and waves back to shore. Breakers tipped the boat sideways and pushed it upright again. I could almost hear a collective catch of breath in the throats of the people watching when a wave washed over the boat's bow or pushed the boat sideways from behind. Several times it looked as though the tiny boat was done for. The North Dakotan waved his life jacket frantically, howling as the boat arrived back to shore. A group of campers along with Kevin and I pulled the boat up on the gravel. The Canadians and others spilled out onto the ground and collapsed, too dizzy to stand. Rain spattered mud and sand into their hair. The North Dakotan laughed as if it were the funniest thing he had ever seen. Kevin, the other campers, and I welcomed them with applause. The men from Winnett just sat and ate their burgers, disappointed, I suppose, that they hadn't witnessed disaster.

After the storm passed and the wind died, smoke rose in straight columns from campfires. The lake smoothed out, and the shadows grew long as the sun set. The North Dakotan passed out on the steps of the camp store. After dark everyone, it seemed, turned in early. Kevin and I sat in the trailer with Spike, talking deep into the night. When I went to bed, I thought again of the people I might disappoint by skipping the lake. But anyone who would give me trouble about it hadn't seen what the people in the boat had gone through, what I'd done to get here.

On Monday I helped Kevin with his campground work before we readied to leave. He talked while I cleaned and scrubbed—toilets, campground, and boat hulls for some of the ranchers. He wasn't being lazy, or it didn't seem so. He was just talking, as if he had to get a final ration of chatter before I left. He talked during the drive to the pond and while he set the minnow traps. Then he talked as he counted the weekend's income and made up a bank deposit. This made him the happiest. He'd have to go to the bank, which meant another of his twice-daily trips into Winnett.

When we had finished and roped the canoe to the cab of his tiny pickup, it was too late to drive to Wolf Point. Instead, we went into Winnett and would take off from there the next morning. As we drove that now-familiar stretch of gravel to town, Kevin fell silent for the first time. He dropped me at his boss's warehouse on the edge of town. He went off to drink beer and flirt with the girls. I had told him I needed to get some rest and wanted a quiet night. Plus, I had no interest in drunken seventeen-year-old girls or a bunch of angry young men griping about their lives. Instead, it was good to sit in front of the warehouse with Spike and look out over the sagebrush. The dog lay next to me, sniffing dusty warm breezes easing off the plains. The sun set behind a line of elk that grazed at the top of a hill. The evening sky turned orange and pink, then purple. The night was quiet but for mice that chewed through burlap feed bags piled in the warehouse.

As with all things Kevin, we didn't get around to leaving Winnett until late the next day. I was not sad to see the town disappear in the distance the next morning. I had grown weary of hearing people complain about federal government this and federal regulations that, niggers this and spics that. (It even hurts to write those words.) Maybe boredom ground hatred and xenophobia into some people. Perhaps it was just the way I perceived things, or maybe it was the loss of my uncle. I knew I hadn't met everyone in Winnett, and it was unfair of me to judge. A small town is more than the sum of a few of its residents. But those I had heard from made it feel good to be moving again.

11 Staying in Motion

THE DEER AND ANTELOPE BEGAN TO PLAY IN THE EASTERN Montana prairies around sunset. At first I saw them in the distance in the evening's tawny light and shadows. Then they grazed in the bushes and grass on both sides of the road. It wouldn't be long, I thought, before they'd start crossing the road. Kevin drove ninety miles-an-hour, trying to get as far as we could before we'd have to pick our way through the deer. Kevin liked speed, and he had a good time pushing the little truck to eighty miles an hour. Ninety. Ninety five . . . I watched the stars pop into the eastern sky. We were on Montana Highway 200, longest state highway in the United States and possibly one of the loneliest roads in the world. We drove for miles without seeing anyone or encountering another car.

I worried about the boat. If it flipped off at ninety-some miles an hour, it would shatter and spray bits of Kevlar and fiberglass all over the road. My river trip would come to an end. But without wakes and sudden crosswinds from other cars and trucks, the canoe rode well. I reached up and checked its position. We sped over a slight rise, and it lofted a little. It bucked occasionally in a wind but stayed steady.

Then Kevin yelped and slammed the brakes. A line of deer sprang from the ditch and across the road. The canoe pitched down over the hood of the truck. He swerved, but the corner of the front bumper whacked a small fawn. It skid across the pavement with its legs splayed, looking like a fallen ice skater. The truck spun in a circle, but our eyes and heads followed the deer as it flopped into the ditch. The canoe rotated on the cab and bumped down over the passenger door.

We snapped to a stop. The engine was silent. Small sounds seemed loud. Kevin's breath. The shuffle of my feet on the floor. Throat clearing.

"Shitfire," I said.

We stepped from the truck. The space around us was humbling. The engine block ticked with heat. The breeze rustled the grass and smelled of sagebrush and burned rubber.

I felt a deep sense of melancholy. Life was tenuous in these sagebrush hills. Despite one of the world's greatest rivers running through this land, every living thing in it often lived by chance of a rainstorm or puddle of water. In this stark landscape, the fawn hardly stood a chance in the first place. It survived its birth, heat and cold, and scarce food. Then a machine came out of nowhere and took all that away. It seemed unfair and pointless.

Kevin realized that hitting a deer had been inevitable. We could have sped another mile or raced around another curve in the road. We might have driven a hundred miles. But we had played chicken and lost. Kevin kept lifting his glasses and wiping his eyes with the back of his hand. He looked away so I couldn't see.

We searched for the deer along a quarter mile of the weed-choked gully. A lone female deer stood watching in the distance, or at least we thought so. We stopped from time to time, hoping to hear the deer moving in the brush. We wanted it to be alive. We wanted it healed so we could send it back into the hills. We heard only wind. The deer was alone in that ditch.

Without talking, we righted the canoe and checked the ropes. Kevin drove with caution, and silence filled the truck. Tiny knots of buildings called Mosby, Cat Creek, and Sand Springs—not towns or even settlements—stood at road crossings. At each, lone street lamps made the emptiness wider and deeper as darkness fell. We dodged herds of deer all eighty miles on Montana 200 from Winnett to Jordan and stopped at a worn-out, dusty all-night gas station. The man behind the counter of the store was gruff. He wore a ball cap with "MY LAND IS MY LAND" stitched across the front. The coffee was awful.

Wolf Point shined, a blanket of lights draped over the hills. Taking a room at a cheap motel, we collapsed and slept hard until 4:00 a.m., when the alarm startled us out of bed. Kevin had to drive me to the riverfront and get back to his job before his boss found out he had left.

A rusty chain and padlock hung on the gate at the entrance to Bridge Park. Montana Highway 13 crossed the Missouri on an old steel-truss structure that creaked and banged under truck wheels. We followed a deep set of tracks around the locked gate. Neat rows of trees bordered an overgrown meadow that spread down to a cottonwood grove down at the river. Grass grew two feet tall around swings, seesaws, and barbecue grills. Broken limbs lay on the roofs of picnic shelters and on tables. Weeds and tree saplings grew in the open spaces of a horseshoe court. One of the ten pits, however, was as clean and trimmed as any in a big-city park. Someone mowed the grass and raked the sand around the stakes. Next to that particular pit, a canopied porch swing swayed in the breeze. Beside the swing rested a glass coffee table and a freestanding ashtray about two feet high.

The park was remote from town and quiet but for an occasional car on the bridge. In the dark before dawn, we unloaded my things by the river and walked up to sit on the porch swing. We smoked a couple of my cigars. He said nothing, and I could tell he didn't want me to go. After he returned to his campground at the lake, he faced a kind of loneliness that forced him into frenzied drives between the lake and Winnett, where he built a superficial social world for himself. He put his cigar out in the ashtray. We said a quick goodbye. I missed him already.

As his truck bumped around the gate, I spread my sleeping bag under a sycamore by a boat ramp. Lying there, I looked at the stars between the leaves. At the top of the opposite bank, people talked and laughed. They'd built a campfire there. I was self-conscious and restless. I wished I was alone to listen to the wind in the trees. To distract myself, I began imagining sunrise throwing shadows across the open meadow. As I fell asleep, I thought I heard horseshoes ringing. Men laughed and chattered in my dream. Once in a while one of them raised his voice to make a point.

The metallic ring of the shoes against the stakes echoed under the canopy of trees, waking me. The morning had grown warm. Men talked and played horseshoes at the trimmed pit. A couple of them sat on the swing. I could hear a riffle on the bank of the river and the pop of an irrigation pump engine in the distance. People on the opposite bank sat together in small groups. Twisted curls of thin blue smoke rose from their fires into the broken light streaming through the trees. A couple of pickups were parked on the road next to the meadow. I watched them out of the corner of my eye as I gathered up my things. A truck door closed, and a Native American woman walked over.

"I'm Val," she said as she approached. She flipped back her long, shiny black hair and held out a soft brown hand. It felt good to take it.

"Val Blackhawk. Whatcha doin'? Mind if I ask?"

She wore a jean jacket. Her T-shirt sagged, and she smelled not unpleasantly of beer and perfume. Her eyes were crystalline, like topaz. The cottonwoods formed an avenue behind her.

"I'm taking this canoe to Kansas City," I said.

"Wow," she said. "I seen a couple of Australians on the river once. It's pretty swift here. My husband went swimmin' off the boat ramp last summer." She pointed with her thumb over her shoulder. A Native American man sat behind the wheel of a truck. He nodded, smiled, and lifted a fan of fingers from the steering wheel. "We hadda pick him up from the other side, downstream a ways," she said. "He ain't such a good swimmer. But my daughters swim here all the time. We got six kids. We're Fort Peck Sioux and live near here on the reservation. It's a nice place."

"You like it, then?" I said.

I was still trying to wake up. I wondered if she opened up to every stranger she met.

"Well, yes we do," she said. "Thanks for askin'. But you might not think it's nice. It ain't much but a tiny house."

"I find nice things everywhere."

"Maybe you'd like it then," she said. "We have our own water, and there's a swing for the kids. My husband and I built a deck on the back, where we can watch the sunset."

"It sounds wonderful," I said. "This park, it's a nice place, too. What about it? It looks closed, but there's people all over."

"Well, no offense or anything," she said, "but the Indians sold it to white men, and the white men closed it."

"No offense at all," I said. "Why did they close it?"

"It was a nice park, good for picnics and parties, ya know," she said, turning and looking at the tables and shelters under the cottonwoods. "But once the Indians sold it, white men ruined it. They didn't like us coming around all night, I guess. And at first, they closed it just at night. Then they closed it all the way, I don't know, to keep us out. Or maybe they ran out of money. It don't matter. We still come here anyway, ya know. Indians, I mean."

Judging from the car tracks worn through the overgrowth, plenty of people came here. At the time, I wanted to ask why the Indians sold the land but thought better of it. I've since discovered that the park closed after the 1993 flood and had not reopened when I came through. Val fed me a line, and I believed her, in part, because I was programmed to. I remember her bright smile and the sparkle in her eye as she told me the story. The Indians–and–white men story formed the germ of a historical tale of cowboys and Indians, of land traded and taken away. I watched her walk back to the truck and climb in with her husband. They smiled and waved. They watched me pack up and were still watching as I set the canoe to the water and drifted into the current.

On the north bank was the Fort Peck Indian Reservation, a two-million-acre stretch of land 110 miles wide and 40 miles from north to south. It was home to seven thousand members of the Sisseton/Wahpeton, Yanktonais, and Teton Hunkpapa Sioux nations and the Canoe Paddler and Red Bottom bands of the Assiniboines. Unemployment plagued Native Americans on the reservation, as did alcoholism and drug abuse, spousal and child abuse. But Gordon Longtree, my Assiniboine friend in Helena, had told me, "Screw it. It's got all the problems you hear about. But we're Fort Peck Indians. Our way doesn't always do things quick. We'll turn out fine if we wait long enough."

The park was about ten miles downstream of the Fort Peck Dam. Upstream of the lake, the river had been turbulent. Sand hit the bottom of the canoe when the water flowed over shoals or curves, and narrows forced the canoe to turn or speed up. The river flowed warm, and its color ranged from deep blue to black and was often opaque. Here, however, the river flowed out of the lake and was wider and smoother than before. It was ice-cold and translucent green blue.

After a calm morning that took me from the treed banks of the park through the plains, the wind increased suddenly, busting off the sagebrush hills. By early afternoon, gusts turned into a steady blast over my bow. The river produced one- to three-foot waves that sprayed over the bow and gave me firm, stinging slaps in the face.

After a while, I relished the challenge the wind gave me. I had gained skill and self-assurance. My shoulders and back had grown stronger and gave me more control of the canoe. As I fought the wind, I wondered if people who drowned here still lay on the bottom and if there were any riverboat wrecks beneath me. I daydreamed of finding one of those wrecks and my fortune in gold dust.

Despite hanging up on numerous sandbars, I made good, steady progress. By late afternoon I had paddled thirty miles in heavy wind. As my stamina ran out, I came into the tight bend at Poplar, a Native American town on the reservation. The river narrowed from about a quarter mile wide to only six hundred feet as it flowed around an island. My forward progress soon ground to a halt. Paddling as hard as I could, I could barely move the boat downstream.

A series of islands and mud banks blocked good access to town until just below a city dump, where I landed and pulled the boat from the water. Around the outskirts of the landfill and the lower end of town, young men wrenched parts out of abandoned cars. They turned, looked me over, and nodded as I walked by. In town, small ramshackle houses of indefinite architecture lined potholed streets of asphalt and dirt. Yards were filled with the detritus of the very poor: tires on rims, wheelless cars, faded plastic toys, rusty bicycles, and heaps of paper and plastic trash. Some houses were obviously abandoned. But the streets were busy with people walking, mainly old men and mothers with children. Many people smiled at me when my eye caught theirs.

At a corner store, the woman at the cash register rang up customers and spent a few moments with each person gossiping about family and neighbors.

"You're pretty new in town, aincha?" she said, when I stepped up with my cola and candy bar. Like her customers, she had flowing black hair, dark eyes, and copper skin.

"I just got here," I said. "I'm traveling."

"No kiddin'," she said. "Well, there's not much in Poplar. Hope you like Indians."

"Yes, thanks," I said. "I certainly do."

"Well, then," she smiled, "you're really gonna like it here."

I asked where I could find the police. I wanted to avoid getting rousted in the middle of the night from my spot down at the river. The station was in a small building. I walked in and asked a woman at a desk if I could talk to an officer. "I hope it's nothing serious," she said, as she stood to go into another room. The police chief, Steve Greyhawk, came out and introduced himself. He was a strong man with broad shoulders, dark eyes, and a face of chiseled bronze angles. He wore the black police uniform of the Assiniboine and Sioux tribal police. An aerial map of Poplar hung on the wall. I pointed to where my boat was.

"Listen, it's all right to camp there, and I'm glad you came in," he said. "But, really, that's a pretty crappy place, it being under the landfill and all. People like to drink there, and they'll keep you up all night. If you don't mind, why don't you pull down here to Max's landing?" He pointed out a place on the bend about a half mile from the canoe. "He has a place behind his trailer out there, and you will be much more comfortable there. There's a little inlet where you're gonna find Max's boat half-sunk. You'll see it."

Max didn't have a phone and was often gone, he said. He rang the donut shop and contacted Max's friend Bob, who was having his afternoon coffee.

"Bob'll take you over to the garage where Max works and get you hooked up," he said, putting down the phone. "He'll be here in a minute. I hope you have a good trip. Enjoy your stay in Poplar and be sure to come see us again."

Bob came into the station a few minutes later. He was white, tall, slender, and dressed in casual slacks and a short-sleeve button-up shirt. We found Max at the garage where he worked and made sure it was all right for me to camp on his place. As Bob and I drove around town, people waved at him. He stopped occasionally and greeted people, and they seemed to be glad to see him. He introduced me as "the new man in town," and they asked if I was there to stay. When I told them I was traveling, several people offered me their couches or spare bedrooms.

All along my journey, white people had cautioned me about Native Americans and Native American towns. In Lander, Wyoming, on the way to Helena, an otherwise kind man who had given me a ride from Lander to Riverton told me I'd better watch out for "drunk and angry" Native Americans on the Wind River Reservation. A woman in Helena had advised me to "run the other way when you see any of those Indians." Another in Great Falls warned, "Them Indians're gonna take whatever you got. I hope you brought your gun." A man in Great Falls said, "Indians won't get off the reservation because the getting there's good. We's the ones paying 'em to lay around. When they do get out and work, they take jobs from guys like me."

None of what these people said about Native Americans turned out to be true. The Native Americans I met on the Wind River Reservation in Helena, and now those in Poplar, were kind. Certainly the town was rough and poor. It had all the problems associated with poverty along with two hundred years of uneven and often arbitrary federal government policy toward Native Americans. Despite their circumstances — or perhaps because of them — these people were outstanding. I'm sure there were drunk Native Americans — there are drunks everywhere. There may have been a few tough guys with chips on their shoulders. But the people I met were, without exception, friendly, open, and generous.

I suspect such generosity has more to do with being poor than with Native culture. I still don't know how to judge such things. But in my experience, those who have the least give the most. Only once on this journey, or on others I've made since, did a person with means offer a ride, a couch, or a cup of coffee. The people who opened their homes to me convinced me that kindness and generosity are universal human qualities. Sometimes heartbreak, disappointment, and bad experience cloud these attributes in some people. Some people connect a negative experience or two with everyone they meet. Others are just bitter or mean. But if I caught them on a different day or a different time in their lives, they might do for me what I would for them.

We rode over to a little restaurant where we met Bob's friend Melvin.

He had blond hair, thick glasses, and bloodshot eyes. He had the restless jitters peculiar to insomnia and boredom. He sat in a booth with his girlfriend's two boys, AJ and Jack. They both had black hair and tawny skin. Their russet eyes were bright and hopeful. Bob and I scooted into their booth. Melvin told me he worked as a computer technician for Assiniboine and Sioux Tribal Industries, a corporation that built metal medical chests and camouflage netting for the armed services.

AJ, the older of the two boys, spoke up: "You came all the way from Kansas City?"

"Yeah," I said. "I walked to Helena and then floated here in a canoe."

"That's something else," he said. "When I get outta high school, I'm going to Haskell (Indian Nations University in Lawrence, Kansas). Then I'm moving to Kansas City. I hear it's a nice place. It's pretty big, and lots to do."

"That's true," I said, "but a lot of Kansas Citians dream of moving away. Home is never as attractive as someplace else."

"I'll give you that," AJ said with a smile. "Here is pretty good, just not enough to do, you know. I bet there's a lot to do in Kansas City. I can't wait to get there."

"Won't you miss it here?"

"Sure," he said. "I'll miss Melvin and my mom. I'll miss Indians."

"We have Indians in Kansas City," I said.

"Yeah, but not like here. This place has Indians like you have white people, I bet."

"That's true, too," I said.

"I'll miss being around Indians, you know, like all the time. But I'll get used to it."

"Do you know what you want to study?" I asked.

"Indian law," he said. "I want to be an Indian lawyer."

"Wow, that's great. Complicated stuff."

"Yeah, but law is how the United States put us Indian people where we are, you know, poor and isolated. I think I can do a lot of good for Indians."

"In Kansas City?"

"The eighth federal district court is in St. Louis, but what Indian wants to live there? Or San Francisco. That's the ninth."

"You seem to know a lot," I said.

"Heck, I'm an Indian."

Melvin ran his hand through AJ's hair and looked up. "If you don't mind," he said, "I'm going with some friends to Wolf Point tonight for dinner. It would be great if you guys could join us."

Bob and I went for coffee and sat in the town park, an open square of grass with picnic tables and grills next to the highway, U.S. 2, the main road through the reservation. Every now and then a car zipped by. Beyond was open prairie. Big oak trees lined the streets of the neighborhood next to us. White and Native children rode bicycles. Some boys played softball on a diamond in the park. Bob told me he had lived in Poplar since the 1960s. He was a retired engineer, a widower.

"I like Poplar plenty," he said. "But there're times when you're faced with Indian ways. It's frustrating. There's such a thing as Indian time, you know. Things happen when they do. You can't get bent out of shape when they don't. But mostly I like it here. It isn't always a picnic, but no place is. Here, at least, I know everybody. The bad guys and the good guys and . . . well, they're my bad guys and my good guys."

We listened to the kids play. They thwacked softballs and squealed on slides and the jungle gym. We sat there a long time conversing and then even longer in silence. When the sun touched the horizon, he took me back to the canoe, bumping down through the dump to the river bank. He watched as I pushed off and fought the murderous wind to get into the current.

As Steve said, Max's boat lolled half-sunk in the green water of a tiny inlet. I pulled the canoe up onto a rise above the boat and waited for Melvin to pick me up for dinner. The river roiled, and the trees and willows on the island across the way whipped in the wind. The last of the sunset shined through the trees and reflected in creamy orange and purple off the river. After dark the wind died. The sounds of train whistles and frogs croaking and clicking echoed along the river bank.

Melvin pulled up in Max's driveway and honked. We drove out to where he worked in a couple of flat industrial buildings. He was proud of what the tribal corporations were doing there. At the same time, he complained of some of the same things Bob had.

"It's hard to run a business here," he said. "The tribes don't want to prop up something that loses money forever. But we have to be an employment agency for the reservation. There's very little brain power for new innovations, and most of our Indian intellectual muscle comes out of Fort Peck Community College or Haskell University, out by you. There's not much of that, either. So the Indians hire people who want to make sure these things work. Like me. By hook and crook, we make camouflage netting, and we get Defense Department contracts for some other things. But there isn't much outside the oil business around here."

We stood in the parking lot. Melvin turned and said he was lonely, despite a girlfriend and two young kids to keep him company.

"AJ was right," he said. "There isn't much to do in Poplar but work and hang out with a few friends. I don't have any hobbies, nothing I'm really interested in but managing this plant. I worry all the time. I have to keep people working, but money's always tight."

He seemed restless and anxious. He reminded me of being stuck in my tent on the lake.

We picked up Bob and drove to a hotel restaurant in Wolf Point and met Russell, a Native farmer. He was a tall man with wide shoulders and large, strong hands. He had a warm, friendly face with intense black eyes.

"The farm is a good place," he said, with a dreamy look in his eye. "I have it mostly in wheat and beans, do a little crop rotation on about a thousand acres, some of which is mine, some I lease."

During dinner the men displayed a special camaraderie and didn't mind inviting me into their discussions of their challenges. Russell related how rocky his marriage had become since the men last met. Melvin commiserated. He had been married once before and told how rough things had become before his divorce. Bob's wife had died several years before. Married life wasn't always great, he said. Sometimes it was just awful "for years running. But I still miss her."

"Yeah, I think I know," Russell said. "I'd do just about anything to keep this marriage together, except give up farming." He picked up a spoon, which seemed comically small in his meaty hands, and rolled it between his fingers. "The ups and downs of growing wheat in dry country, that's more important. It's what keeps life focused."

They spoke to me in personal terms — the way people who trust but don't know each other do. If I lived alongside these men, our relationships would wax and wane and grow in different directions, and perhaps we wouldn't be so open with each other. But that's the nature of having a traveler around, someone you know can't hurt you because they will go away.

Melvin left me off at Max's landing, where I sat under a vault of starlight. Cool air came up off the water. Coyotes yipped and howled on the other side of the river. A million frogs squeaked and whistled.

Shortly after I'd made myself comfortable, Max walked down to the landing and asked me if I wanted to come inside. He fluffed his mop of unkempt blond hair and squinted through thick glasses. He looked down at his feet, avoiding my eyes.

"I can't sleep," he said. "I wouldn't mind watching TV with someone. I mean, being on the river and all, you can't see much news. You think it's something you'd like to do?"

"Sure," I said. "I'd like that."

His trailer was the small, crowded space of a loner. He'd hung his walls full with pictures of his two kids and former wife. He kept his high school track trophies in neat rows on a dusty shelf. Newspapers and celebrity magazines littered tabletops and the floor. A pile of to-go boxes from chain restaurants teetered atop a wastebasket. An open trail through it all led from the bedroom through the kitchen to the couch.

Max was glad to have company. He talked about his kids. One lived on her own, and the other split time between her mother and him. He read about celebrities, he said, because he dreamed of a life of ease.

"People say all the time money doesn't solve your problems," he said. "But them that're saying it are trying to make themselves feel better about not having any. I work all the time and can't save nothing between child support and other bills. Can't fix my boat. It sunk in there last year. Just for once, I'd wanna be unhappy and have pocket fulla money. I'd like to know what that's like."

After a few minutes, he turned on his twelve-inch black-and-white television. We looked at weather and news until I began to nod.

I excused myself. As I stood, he offered me a jug of cold water from his refrigerator.

"Take this," he said. "It's going to be hot tomorrow, and if you keep this on the bottom of the boat, it'll stay cool until you drink it up."

Before getting into my tent, I watched the stars awhile and thought about this remarkable place. The mark of a town or a place wasn't its wealth or poverty. It wasn't race or ethnicity. It wasn't how much business it did, how many churches it had, or how many people belonged to the Oddfellows, Boy Scouts, or Chamber of Commerce. A place revealed itself by how its people treated each other and how they, in turn, treated strangers. Despite Poplar's problems, its people, the ones I met, cared for each other and welcomed me into their lives. When I came up out of the dump, no one knew me or could tell me from any other stranger. I was just a grubby white guy in shorts and a T-shirt.

Frankly, I could see why someone would want to live in Poplar and, just as clearly, why they'd want to leave. The people I'd met were bored, dreaming of other places or distant goals: AJ wanted to be a lawyer in the big city. Melvin sought commercial success and the approval of his Native American neighbors. Bob was glad when he could have a conversation with someone who wasn't from Poplar. Max was a ne'er-do-well, but he came by his trailer and half-sunken boat honestly. He wasn't dreaming of going anywhere.

Since that night in Poplar, I've met hundreds of Bobs, Melvins, Russells, and Maxes. Men and women lose their mates and find equilibrium in places that gave them little challenge. Melvin wasn't just a man I knew in a little town once. He's everyone who ever stood still until boredom and loneliness drove them to do something—anything—to end the misery. Then there are people who find all the purpose and meaning they need in their work, and those who have settled for what life has given them, and that's enough.

But AJ, that silky-haired kid who imagined a great life for himself in Kansas City, sticks in my mind. I hope he achieved his dreams. As a college professor and ironworker, I meet AJs all the time. Ironworkers and students alike imagine futures in great careers and adventurous lives. The look in their eyes resembles something between daydreaming and epiphany. They peer over the horizon at places so much better, brighter, and more interesting than where they are. Young ironworkers ask me about the places I've been, the languages I speak, and what living in a canoe or out of a backpack is like. In the process of freeing themselves from their parents, students discover my past. Some seek me out, as if I have the wisdom of the ages. I advise them to look inside themselves for the inspiration they seek. All of them work like animals—hanging beams and carrying rebar, studying for exams or avoiding learning anything—because their lives really do depend on staying in motion. If the movement stops, they might do things other people always told them they couldn't.

This past semester, I had a student in my American history course with that restless, faraway look in her eyes. She came to every class but turned in no assignments. She flunked all the tests. I asked her to come to my office to talk about her grades. When she arrived, she told me right off that she liked hearing my lectures but had no interest in school.

"I thought I'd get the hang of school once I started," she said. "But I didn't. I'm just filling my time. What I really want is to . . ."

She was self-conscious, reticent to say what came next.

"Go on," I said. "It's all right."

"I really just want to pack my bag and walk out the front door."

I told her what I tell my daughter: "Careers are like toasters, blenders, and microwaves. You think you need them, but you don't. Not now, anyway. And they'll be there when you want them. So, go. You'll be afraid. That's part of the deal. You'll find yourself among hostile people sometimes. You'll have to be resourceful. But you'll never know what's on the other side of the road if you don't cross it."

After high school, Sydney decided to travel. She went to Europe and had a terrible time. She was fearful and felt isolated. Later, she worked in Yellowstone National Park and learned a great deal. These days, she goes to college on and off, confident that school will be there when she wants it. She says she's thinking about leaving town again next summer for "who knows where." She wants to go to Europe again, having learned something of herself. Yellowstone, perhaps, or Mexico. Good for her.

Maybe college teachers and fathers shouldn't counsel their charges to abandon conventional life and go where they need to go. Staying on the beaten path is easier. There's less heartbreak and more security. But remembering that deer Kevin and I smacked with his truck in central Montana, I send those students out of my office with one admonition: "You're going to get walloped, right out of the blue. It'll set you back, make you scared. But take a deep breath and stand up again. Your discoveries will be worth the pain."

I recently received a postcard from my former student. It's here on the desk next to my computer. After school this year, she hitchhiked through the Midwest into New England and on to Prince Edward Island.

"It's brilliant," she writes.

12 Owl Headdress

THE DAY I LEFT MAX BEHIND, I COULD ONLY THINK OF HOW it must feel to be unhappy and rich, not unhappy and poor. Money may not solve all my problems, I thought, but it solves the problem of being poor.

After grad school in Wyoming, I returned to Kansas City but couldn't find a job. Reflecting on that time, I find reasons employment eluded me. Even though I was looking in the right places, master's degrees in history weren't in high demand in 1993. I was anxious, needy, and in way over my head. Nothing flushes away chances of employment quicker than desperation. I possessed no job-interview skills or even the kind of résumé that comes out of the middle of the stack and snags an interview. More important, I didn't know what I wanted to do. I only wanted money in my pocket and confidence in my heart, both conditions that had never plagued me.

Being jobless wasn't so bad. I'd received an insurance settlement from a car crash. Walking around with a busted-up body wasn't worth the money, but the settlement took me through the summer and gave me tons of time with Sydney. We drew, sculpted, and assembled collages from magazines and construction paper. She told me stories, and I wrote them down for her. We played in parks, went to museums, and picnicked in the living room. From the front porch swing, we watched the sun set trees afire in afterglow. We visited friends and went to the ice-cream shop. I hefted her up on my shoulders and walked through neighborhoods and down Kansas City's boulevards. We walked at night and sometimes very early in the morning before the neighborhood came awake. Sydney tells me today that her first memories of Kansas City are from seven feet in the air.

Employment is way overrated, I think. But the problem with unemployment is that it doesn't and can't last long enough, unless you have money. And mine was running out.

I found a job in banquet service at the Kansas City Ritz-Carlton. I worked with fine, sociable people who were interesting and funny. It was boom and bust—sometimes seasonal and always dependent on convention business. But in a few months, I built a bank account on it. After child support and rent, I had a little left over for special things for Sydney—a hamburger at a local restaurant, an extra ice-cream cone, and a new toy now and then.

But I'm a strong starter who bores of a job or new skill in short order. I'm that guy who shows up at the job, makes a big splash, and then disappears after just a few months. After years of intensive research, I've concluded that my shelf life at a job is about six months. Then I sit around rotting, until the misery becomes too great and I make my next move.

Fortunately, the hotel's lead engineer discovered I could refinish and repair antiques—a skill I'd gained working with an independent craftsperson years before. I moved from serving tables to refinishing the antique and reproduction furniture in the public areas of the 360-room hotel. It was great fun, as is any new endeavor. After just a few months, however, my enthusiasm flagged. I did good work but found the routines increasingly poisonous. Soon I had difficulty getting out of bed in the morning. At the end of the day, I was too tired for walks with Sydney. I dreamed of other places as I sanded a Queen Anne maple chest or lacquered a Louis XVI bronze-gilt commode. I dwelled on past mistakes and disappointments and all the things I might have done.

Max bothered me, because we were so much alike. Even our houses resembled each other. I hung past joys and bygone accomplishments on the wall. My possessions were meager—we both owned the same brand and model black-and-white television. I kept my house neater; and any trophies I earned, I'd thrown away. Still, Max and I were ghosts. We inhabited the same ill-defined space. We sought significance but remained anonymous. We longed for an easier life. Neither of us had much to say, even if we covered that fact up in different ways. I talked all the time; he said almost nothing. We had no wives. Our kids split their time between houses. We worked at jobs that made no difference to anyone anywhere.

When I started out from Kansas City, I thought I wanted an escape from the grinding routines of daily life. In the plains and on the river, I'd prove myself to me and to everyone else. Then, I believed, my newfound knowledge would make my work easier and fatherhood just dandy. But as I paddled through the expansive countryside east of Poplar, I realized just how passive Max and I were. We expected that one great stroke of genius, lightning strike, or lottery ticket would rescue us. He sat in his trailer and waited for things to change on their own. I waited for the trip to give me all I needed.

I pushed a paddle into the river, and the river drove my thoughts into niches and facets of my personality I'd never explored and many I'd ignored. At home I used television and radio, music and friends as distractions. If I didn't turn up the radio, I worked harder, ran or cycled farther, or talked louder. Stepping off my porch, I'd walked away from these distractions. Rural highways allowed me to think. They made me think. I experienced and felt my insides, because nothing distracted me from it. The river, however, gave me solitude unlike any I had ever known. In doing so, it compelled me to contemplate my life, present and past. The turn inward happened incrementally, slowly, without my ever noticing. Until I paddled away from Max, I didn't understand I'd embarked on a journey of self-discovery far longer and larger than any one trip can be.

After paddling many miles from Poplar, I lay back in my canoe and watched the clouds race overhead. I'd left the mean, spiteful woman at Wolf Creek three weeks before. In that time, I paddled three hundred miles in a little over two weeks and spent the rest of the time with Kevin at Crooked Creek. My canoeing skill had grown to the point where I maneuvered the canoe on the water as I wished and set it ashore where I wanted. I'd lived through all kinds of situations. Even fighting the wind, paddling up and down swells on the lake, and raw boredom did not lessen my resolve to complete what I had started.

I stared at a sky so blue it hurt. The river flowed fat and steady, meandering in snakelike curves over its floodplain. Four river miles looped from one set of yellow-and-red striated sandstone bluffs to the other and back but advanced only a mile or so as the crow flies. The river took me through farms and ranches in the wide river bottoms. Along the banks, some landowners stacked hundreds of junked cars, tires, and refuse to keep the Missouri from washing away their real estate. I paddled, napped, and paddled some more. All I remember of the towns of Brockton and Culbertson were water towers standing up in the prairies. Near Culbertson, sandbars fluttered like birds' wings across the river, dividing the channel into braids. Pelicans and cormorants grunted, squealed, and croaked. Toward dusk the wail of a common loon echoed down the river. There is no sound more lonely, haunting, and beautiful.

Toward sunset a wind came up suddenly. I came around a bend and directly into where it rocketed out of a trough in the bank that had once been the river channel. Brush and small trees in there thrashed like whips. Beyond the old channel, a rainbow opened full across the sky. Paddle as I might, I came to a standstill alongside a bluff of hard-packed clay and loess. A slide had formed a small cup about twenty feet above the river. The ground above it looked like it might give out again in a solid rain. The opposite bank promised even less. The river bent around acres of mud pocked with knots of grass and cattail spikes.

I was tired. Despite the dangers of camping on such unstable ground, I dragged the canoe up the bank and set the tent up in the shelf. From there, I could see miles into the valley on the opposite bank. The land spread out in deepening tones of red and brown toward the setting sun. I sat and watched the sky for a long time. The cup of tea I'd made after pitching the tent turned cold in my hand. Slowly the stars chased the last of the sunlight from the sky. The wind eased some, and the gnats and mosquitoes drove me into the tent. Wind rattled in the cottonwood leaves until long after dark.

The night disappeared in a blink. Sunrise tinged the yellow bluffs and eerie badlands orange. Over the next fifty-five miles, my longest day yet, blue-and-black streaks of coal and shale showed through the yellow strata of the hills. The river now wound miles around a hill or spit of land to curl back a quarter mile or less from itself. It didn't straighten until well into afternoon. Then the wind dropped off, and gnats gathered in clouds around the canoe. They zipped in my nose and ears and landed on the edges of my eyes. I paddled faster to create a headwind and put miles and miles behind me.

Late in the evening, I beached on a small gravel bank that gave way to a steep embankment about eight feet high. Above, a field of neatly trimmed grass spread up to groves of sycamores and elms. "Someone mowed the grass for me!" I thought. As I pulled my gear from the canoe, a small herd of sheep ran across the meadow and began to follow my every step. As I explored the peninsula where this meadow stood, the flock grew to several dozen dirty fluffs. I walked and they walked. I stopped and they gathered around me. I ran from them and they raced to catch up. I had grown up with storybooks full of gentle, dumb, and loveable sheep. But there were also horses in those books; and every time I had gotten on a horse, it bit me. What were sheep capable of? I'd never heard of them trampling anyone to death; but until a horse took a chunk of flesh off my leg when I was eleven, I'd never heard of horses eating people either.

I elbowed sheep away from my pack stove so I could make a cup of tea and boil some rice. Then I dove into my tent, hoping it would hold back a stampede. The fear of sheep squashing me under hoof kept me awake until late. Around midnight I regretted not being able to see the sky and snuck out for a cigar and gander at the stars.

The sheep had disappeared.

Since I put in the river past Wolf Point, the sounds of machinery, cars, and trains had injected sonic clutter into what was once almost perfect quiet. Irrigation pumps whirred. Water intakes slurped. Tractors thrummed. Downstream about two hundred yards from where I camped, a truck bumped over an old lift bridge that I could just make out in the light of the rising moon. Long-unused cables attached to two large groups of pulleys affixed high on either end of the bridge, like fists bent in on upraised forearms. Beyond it, an oil rig's engine popped. The whine of tires on pavement washed over the landscape.

In the morning a flock of five hundred bleating, grass-chewing, hoof-tromping sheep milled around the tent. Everything — my tent, sleeping bag, clothes — smelled of dirt, sheep urine, and sheep sweat. I poked my head out. Their little turds blanketed the ground. They wedged up around the tent so closely that I couldn't get out. I talked to them, tried to reason with them. I pleaded with them and yelled at them. They didn't move. They looked as if they wanted something. And I couldn't believe how big sheep could be. Their heads came up to my shoulders. They weren't guanacos or llamas. Maybe they weren't sheep either, I thought, but genetic experiments. What if there were shepherd dogs? What would they make of me? Would they bite?

I told myself, "They're just fucking sheep!" and bullied out among them. Elbowing and shoving, I opened up a little spot in the crowd. I flapped my arms and yelled, "Git! Go on. There's nothing here!" They watched calmly and gave only a little space for me to get the tent down. When, by some miracle, I had my things packed, I shouldered, pushed, and butted the whole length of the meadow to the canoe. When I pushed off, I still couldn't escape. My clothes, bags, canoe — everything — smelled like sheep and sheep pee and sheep dung.

Under the bridge, a man sat on the steep bank, a fishing pole in his hands and a cooler at his side. I wondered how he avoided the sheep. I nearly asked, but he got me first. "Hallo, there, young man," he yelled, his voice booming under the tangle of metal cables and beams. "Where're you going in that boat?" I told him I was headed for Kansas City. He sat silent for a moment. "A fine thing it is to be free, floating on a river," he said. "You're one lucky man."

Yes, it was true, I thought. It was good to be free of the constraints of society and livestock. It was good to be on a river. Even better, I thought, was to know the Missouri not just as a path to freedom, but as freedom itself.

I canoed another four or five miles out of Montana and into North Dakota. I planned to stop at Fort Union and was excited to see the National Park Service reproduction of John Jacob Astor's American Fur Company fur-trading post. Established in 1828, Fort Union became the center of trade in bison hides and beaver skins with the Assiniboines to the north, the Crows of Yellowstone, and the Blackfeet who lived in the area above what was now Fort Peck Lake. At its peak in the 1840s and 1850s, the tiny fort employed a hundred people with a palisade-protected yard, complete with gunners' posts, stores, livery, and living quarters. The post operated for thirty-nine years, when finally Indian trouble, change in fashion, and extirpation of the bison and beaver in the area — the grizzlies and black bears and mountain lions had been hunted out decades before — ended the fur trade.

Because I didn't really know what Fort Union looked like, I paddled right past it and landed downstream on a low, muddy bank choked with weeds, tall water grasses, cattails, and willows. I figured, after a short jaunt through the mud, I'd step out of the weeds and into the fort. I slipped on my sneakers and tucked my boots under my arm. (I went barefoot in the canoe.) Parting the cattails and eight-foot-high grass, I stepped out of the canoe and sunk into deep, stinking muck. The wetland stretched out over a mile before the ground firmed up and a cattle trail opened in the tangle. It was jungle hot. The humidity stifled my breathing. Once out of the cattails, I saw the fort another mile in the distance.

By the time I reached the post, I was a sweaty mess, covered with muck, sweat, grass seed, and cattail fluff. I rubbed my legs against the dry grass and changed my shoes. Still striped in mud, I stepped into the crisp air-conditioning of the small, sparkling-clean museum.

I don't remember much about the museum. The sun had cooked my brain, and mushing knee-high through the wetland made me weary. The post superintendent also communicated that he didn't appreciate dirty river travelers in his museum.

I was puzzled. I found myself with no interest in the museum or the artifacts it housed. As a kid, I'd dreamed of the fort, imagining myself as a fur trader who lived among the Native Americans. Karl Bodmer's paintings of the fort captivated me. The paintings and sketches of Swiss artist Rudolf Friedrich Kurz, along with his journals, were the stuff of adventure. Edwin Denig, the manager of the post in the 1850s, wrote accounts of life among the Assiniboines and the other Native Americans of the Upper Missouri. And here I was, without one drop of fascination. I milled around the exhibits at the main house, trying to reignite my enthusiasm. But nothing came of it. I was too hot and tired to care much about anything.

Instead, I asked the persnickety ranger if I could use the phone. At the

Crooked Creek Recreation Area, the fun-loving, risk-immune, drunken North Dakotan told me, even begged me, to call his cousin when I landed at Fort Union. He was in a sober, if hungover, moment the morning after he perched himself at the bow of the Canadians' boat. I said I would. As he scrawled the number in my journal, he said he'd call her and tell her all about me. "She's gonna love you," he said. "I swear to God."

When I rang, DelRae Steinbeisser had no idea what I was talking about. She hadn't heard from her cousin in months.

"It doesn't matter," she said. "The kids and I are looking to get out of here. I'll bring lunch, something that won't drag you down in the sun. Salad or something. You like sweet stuff?"

"I'd kill for sweet stuff," I said.

"Sit tight."

She arrived an hour later in a big white pickup with her two boys. Jack, a border collie, barked and wagged its tail so hard its butt wagged with it. DelRae was a broad-shouldered woman, tall and strong. She was about thirty years old; wore jeans and a sleeveless shirt; and had sun-bleached, shoulder-length red hair. Without hesitation, she told me to get into the truck. She shook my hand and welcomed me to North Dakota.

We drove to Fort Buford, a state of North Dakota historic site that had been an army post during the American Indian Wars. The buildings of the then-defunct Fort Union provided the army with lumber to construct the main buildings of Fort Buford.

It was good to talk with DelRae. Her cheerful attitude and bright personality were just what I needed after being alone for a few days. We sat on the tailgate of her pickup in the shade of a big cottonwood next to an irrigation ditch. She'd brought a big salad, along with bread, fruit, and lots of homemade chocolate-chip cookies. Jack jumped in and out of the thick grass, and the kids played tag in mowed grass on the other side of the road.

"Funny, you calling today," she said. "I didn't have much planned but dinner tonight. I sure wish you'd come up and have dinner with us, stay the night."

I told her I'd like to but that time was weighing on me. I wanted to see my daughter, I told her. But I didn't want to go home. Life on the river was too good, even in its worst moments. I really didn't know what I needed or wanted from a job. I only knew I didn't want one. I didn't want more routines. I wanted no obligations beyond just setting my daughter on my shoulders and walking wherever our hearts took us. I'd never known anything but work, I said. Even in my many travels, I'd gotten jobs along the way to make ends meet. Going back to Kansas City meant that I would have to work for others. The thought of it made me sad.

"That's too bad for me," she said. I must have looked at her like I'd lost track of the conversation.

"You leaving today, I mean," she continued. "I hear what you're saying about a job and work. My God! I'd like to talk more about it. And I think you'd like my family. We live on a farm about fifteen miles south of here. It's a nice place, couple of cows on the yard with more on acres and acres of grazing land. We have wheat, too, but we lease most of that out. We have plenty of room; and the way the boys get on with you, I'm sure they would love to have you."

We ate slowly, talking about farm life, the Steinbeisser family, and some of the things she hoped to do someday.

"I wouldn't mind going to college some more," she said. "I've looked into it and think I might begin next year. But who knows—the farm might fall apart if I were to get a little education. And I think it might be a good thing, too."

"Good thing?"

"Yeah, you know, we find out a new way to keep ourselves afloat that we like better."

"Any idea what you'd like to study?"

"I was thinking of history," she said.

"I love history," I said. "I have a master's in history."

"Really," she said. "There's so many jobs in history these days, historians are taking to the river?"

"Well, yeah," I said laughing. "I thought I'd do a little research with a canoe paddle."

"Well, I don't know why you studied history," she said, "but, to me, the past is just interesting. Stuff like who we were and how we got to be who we are. But before I can go to school, there are some things I need to get out of the way. I'm pretty good at math, so that wouldn't be so hard. But I am not sure about those English classes. I'm not much of a writer."

"I don't think those English papers should worry you much," I said. "If you go into history, you'll get plenty of practice. Writing's all historians do when they aren't on rivers."

We drove up to the post cemetery. Rows of whitewashed wooden grave markers formed neat lines in the grass. A local historical association had re-created the originals for the tourists. A name was scribed on each of the markers. Some had death dates and causes of death: "Killed by Indians," alcoholism, consumption, inebriation, meningitis, Bright's disease (kidney disease), "Died in a fight," exposure, cholera, dysentery, smallpox, "Froze to death."

We rambled a long time among the markers, talking about the common and uncommon names on them and the causes of death. Among the Native Americans, soldiers, and wives and children, two in particular caught my eye:

Son of Owl Headdress, 1870, Jan. 5, disease
Owl Headdress, 1870, Feb. 5, beat to death

I read a sad story in those markers, one that I discovered years later had no basis in fact. Owl Headdress wasn't in that graveyard. He was born in 1842 and served in the U.S. Army at Fort Buford. During military exercises, cannon flash partially blinded him. The army gave him a discharge. Being Native American, however, he received no benefits or compensation for his injury. He lived until 1908. When U.S. Highway 2 was constructed in the 1950s, his family moved his remains out of the right-of-way to a cemetery near Wolf Point. In the late-1990s Owl Headdress's great-grandson, Sheldon Headdress, agitated for a proper military burial for the old soldier. In 2001 the army marked his grave with a military headstone. The Veterans of Foreign Wars gave him a twenty-one-gun salute. I have yet to find anything definitive about his son.

That day at Fort Buford, I was pensive, despite my companion and her bubbly brood. At the time, I suspected that the fort was a reconstruction for tourists, which was, in part, true. When the fort closed in 1895, the military moved the dead to the Custer National Cemetery at Little

Big Horn. The original wooden grave markers rotted away. The state historical society reconstructed the ones that DelRae and I saw. To me, it was all just letters on wood. As we walked away, I thought how these markers would disappear in time and these people would cease to be tourist attractions. Then, I thought, they would rest in peace.

The boys and I played fetch with Jack until it came time for them to move on. Before they did, DelRae wanted to show me where I could stay the night. We drove down to a campground across from the mouth of the Yellowstone, just a few miles downstream of where I'd stowed my boat. Cottonwood and ash trees grew in long lines along the bank, disappearing in a haze in the distance. The Yellowstone drew a wide arc of deep blue in the Missouri's cloudy green water. Bird songs and the whine of tires on the highway broke the silence.

DelRae offered to put the canoe and gear in the back of the truck. She promised she'd bring me back the next day or a few days on, depending on how long I wanted to stay. Again I told her that I felt a draw toward home and needed to keep moving. She drove me back to Fort Union and dropped me off near the front door.

"I would really love to join you," I said. She gave me a hug, and I shook the boys' hands.

"Too bad for us. You call or come by anytime you want."

By the time I was on the river, the weather threatened wind and storm. There was only one trailer at the campground when I arrived, grandparents and their granddaughter. They had an old sports boat made of wood with "Miranda" painted across the sides. I set camp and made dinner. While I was eating, the grandfather came over to chat.

Jim Ross was a big man with catcher's mitt hands, strong and calloused. He wore thick horn-rimmed glasses and spoke slowly and deliberately.

"We camp here all the time," he said. He stuffed his hands in the pockets of his jeans and stood rock steady as he talked. "It's a good place to get away from the farm and spend some time on the rivers with the boat. We can go a piece up the Yellowstone before we hit a diversion dam. And we can go anywhere on the Missouri. It's a fine river. The best."

Rain began. Jim invited me into his trailer. We sat under a comfortable light at a large window. His granddaughter played with a feisty beagle on the floor. Jim's wife sat at a little couch, reading.

"I was here once when the ice broke on the Yellowstone," Jim said. "Early spring. Both rivers were still iced over real good. There had been a rain upstream on the Yellowstone, a real drencher, and the water backed up behind the ice. We hear this huge crack and a buncha little ones, kinda like fireworks but louder. Sheets of ice higher than this camper come sliding up the bank. They piled up like books. It got louder than a freight train. It was a sight."

We looked out on where the Yellowstone met the Missouri. The river was over a half mile wide at the confluence. Rain had come and gone and come again. The sun was low and beamed up beneath the blue-black clouds, lacing them with orange filament. On my way to Helena, the Yellowstone I'd seen in the national park had been savage—a rocky, whitewater stream. But here on the plains, it flowed flat and smooth. It ruffled the Missouri as it flowed into it.

Jim's ranch, he said, was about fifty miles to the west and south of the river near Enid, Montana. He talked about his farm and how it worked, as if he really just wanted to talk; and talking to a stranger gave him a break from his wife and grandchild. He raised livestock, which, since I knew nothing of "the livestock," was interesting. More fascinating, however, was his passion for his cows.

"I raise pure-blood Simmentals," he said, "a breed strong and hardy for this extreme climate here in Montana. And it produces good beef, good-tasting beef. I do well, as I don't inoculate or hormone up my cattle to get 'em strong and big enough for winters. I'm not an organic farmer but almost. I hardly use any antibiotics. A Simmental is like that."

While we talked, his granddaughter, who was about ten, made us s'mores and lolled with the beagle on the floor of the trailer. We talked about kids and grandkids, camping, boating, and fishing. When we looked out the window again, night had fallen.

I walked away from the trailer feeling good after our long conversation. The rivers glowed under the stars. I sat at a picnic table by my tent and stared over the rivers. They looked still and calm. But I knew that beneath that appearance they were strong, chaotic, and persistent in their struggle with one another.

The coyotes yipped in the river bottom on the opposite bank. The Missouri itself lived. It threw driftwood against bridge pilings and piers and gave shelter to all kinds of life. Fish flopped along the banks. Groundhogs burrowed in the levees, and beavers built lodges in backwaters. A bawling yawp raised clouds of bank swallows from beneath bridges. The river changed with the season. In the summer heat and haze, it buzzed with the whine of cicadas and tires on the highways. It sang with birds and hummed and banged with the sounds of the cities. In winter, ice floes big as cars slushed against one another, larger pieces thundering as they shattered in the distance. I used to imagine that I could jump from one piece of ice to another all the way across the river. Spring's rains and the summer melt put all manner of organic matter into it, from the tiniest sticks to living cottonwoods. Floods sent people sandbagging. It was a heroic stream then, a once-quiet worker who rose up, demanded attention, and refused to be taken lightly.

Investing my personal being and energy in the Missouri, I came to know it intimately. The boundaries between it and me became fuzzy, gray, and incredibly deep and complex. I was a part of the river as much as it was of me. I shaped it, and it shaped me, in a relationship that will continue until I die.

If I become something else after I die, our relationship will continue then, perhaps, for eternity.

I tossed and turned all night. I wanted, needed to see my daughter. I looked forward to the company of my friends. But I didn't want to lose contact with the river and the life I built on it. I did not long for the comforts of home. In them, I feared, I would find purgatory. More than ever, that seemed worse than perdition.

I wished I had a million dollars.

13 Doris

THE YELLOWSTONE DIDN'T FLOW INTO THE MISSOURI. IT collided with the big river. On the south bank, the Yellowstone flowed deep blue and clearer than the Missouri, which ran muddy and green and opaque on the north bank. For several miles, the rivers jostled against each other around a tight bend and then next to each other without coming together as one. As the two rivers fought for space in a common riverbed, the water roiled, splashed, and erupted in boils.

I paddled back and forth across the swells, bobbing, rising, and falling over the boundary where the two rivers elbowed against one another until they slowly, inevitably became the Missouri I knew. Having subsumed the Yellowstone, the Missouri moved more quickly and powerfully, its current potent, determined, and swift. I felt it in my paddle and in the way the canoe slipped sideways over currents spouting up from the depths. The river rolled around big bends and into straight, narrow runs, where it flowed as if through a sluice.

Toward afternoon the Missouri widened and slowed. The water slowly turned from cloudy green to clear blue as the river flowed into Lake Sakakawea. The miles-wide, board-flat bottomland rose into green-and-gray striated bluffs in the distance. The sun was out full, and it was a hot day. The winds increased quickly. I pulled my boat up into the brush near the U.S. Highway 85 bridge into Williston. Waves broke over the stern.

I craved a hot shower and a night in a clean bed. Williston was the first big town on the river since Wolf Point, which lay 120 miles upstream. I had no idea how long it would take to paddle the lake or if there would be any Kevins along the way to break the solitude. Plus, the three-mile walk into town would do me good.

I stashed the canoe out of sight in heavy brush under a long line of trees. The only people who might see my boat were over a half mile away on the other side of what was no longer a river but wasn't quite a lake. Houses there had boat docks, and I figured it was a rare American who would abandon a fancy motorboat for my canoe. And anyone who wanted it deserved it if they braved the tangles of grape, poison ivy, and Virginia creeper to get to it. With a dry bag slung over my shoulder, I whacked, hacked, and stomped my way through those green tentacles until I reached the end of the bridge.

A road from a suburban subdivision met the highway at the top of a hill about a mile from the bridge. A car stood there with the hood up. As I walked by, a man looked up from the engine and smiled.

"You know anything about cars?" he asked. "I don't have a clue."

"Yeah," I said. "Simple things. Nothing too complex."

"If you're at simple, you're way ahead of me," he said.

Rick introduced himself. He had a scruffy beard and moustache, and his hair sprayed beneath a ball cap. He puffed on a pipe.

"This is my father-in-law's car," he said. "He's kind of an older guy, a great guy, but he's never where he says he's gonna be. I've been looking for him in his old haunts for about an hour. I was going to a library down there where he hangs out." He pointed to the houses in the valley below. "Then this happens."

"Why doesn't he have his car?" I said.

"Because he can't see to drive," he said.

I got up under the hood. A fan belt had come loose. We dug around in the trunk and found some tools. I fixed the belt, topped off the radiator from a gallon jug of spring water Rick had picked up from the store, and adjusted the alternator so the belt was tight.

"Thanks," he said, reaching for his wallet. "Let me give you a little money."

"No thanks," I said. "I'd do it for anyone."

I picked up my bag and started down the road. Williston shimmered in the distance. The lake arched around the town, behind which rose white-and-green-layered hills and bluffs. It was a beautiful, spare place, a prairie town. What it didn't have in tall buildings it had in water towers.

I walked downhill, enjoying the feel of pavement beneath my feet for the first time in over a month. Heat ticked off the asphalt and rose in mirages in the distance. I was about a mile from town when Rick pulled up.

"If you won't take my money," he said, "then you'll take a ride, won't you?"

I asked if he could drop me off at a motel.

"Sure, I will," he said. "I know one people say is pretty good. It's cheap and clean. Ride with me while I look for my father-in-law."

I could tell he wanted company. We had a pleasant time poking into libraries and coffee shops looking for his stray father-in-law. He puffed on his pipe and refilled it from time to time. It made me think he didn't or couldn't smoke at home. We drank coffee and ate lunch together. It didn't seem that he was worried about his father-in-law. Instead, he carried an air of resignation, as if he went on this kind of errand often.

Throughout the town, the plastic centers had blown out of motel and grocery store signs. Where colorful advertisements once covered billboards, bits of paper now fluttered. Many of the signs were bent. Others lay over one another in spaghetti-like tangles. I asked Rick what had happened.

"A big storm blew through here a week or so ago," Rick said. "It came down the Missouri. A big deal. Tornadoes and everything."

"Tornadoes?"

"Yep," he said. "It was pretty cool, really. I like big storms. I stand out in my driveway and watch them come in."

"Really," I said. "I'm glad I'm not alone."

"It kinda makes you feel guilty, you know, to enjoy a storm," he said. "Fortunately, this one didn't cause much human damage, so I didn't feel so awful. High winds and stuff tore up these signs and whatnot. You could hear it come down the valley, like droves of fighter planes."

"I was in it, I think," I said. "I camped above the river on Fort Peck Lake. I imagine it was the same storm. A waterspout came up off the lake right in front of me."

"No shit," he said. "How'd you make out?"

"I thought it was going to blow me off the map," I said.

"Good thing it didn't," he said.

"The storm was beautiful."

"Yes, it was," he said.

Rick dropped me at a clean motel that had cable television and a fair price. A long bath took the river grime and sweat off, and I was almost sad to see what the Missouri had given me wash down the drain. But not quite.

In the quiet of the motel room there was nothing to distract me from a dilemma I'd contemplated since Kevin dropped me off at Wolf Point: Fort Peck Lake was 134 miles long, and I could hardly imagine canoeing that lake in the conditions I encountered. Lake Sakakawea put 178 miles of water before me. After that came Lake Oahe, 231 miles; Lake Sharpe, 80 miles; Francis Case, 107 miles; and Lewis and Clark Lake, 25 miles. All together, 621 miles of wind-torn lake stood between me and the last dam on the Missouri at Yankton, South Dakota. If I was to skip it all, including the short stretches that flowed between reservoirs, I would miss about eight hundred miles of the river.

The Corps of Engineers built the reservoirs between the mid-1930s and mid-1960s. Excluding Fort Peck, which was a Depression-era works program, five of the reservoirs were part of the Pick-Sloan Missouri Basin Plan. Nature forced compromise between the corps and the Bureau of Reclamation, which fought each other for decades over control of the Missouri. In 1943 the Missouri flooded after years of drought on the Great Plains. A sudden spring thaw in the Rockies combined with drenching April rains throughout the Missouri's 530,000-square-mile basin, carrying away farmland, houses, and towns the entire 2,300-mile length of the river. In Omaha the river flowed seven feet deep over the city's river-bottom airport. In Kansas City the Missouri flooded the city's industrial East and West bottoms (for the fourth time since 1900). The river rushed into the city's famed stockyards, washing cows, cattle trucks, railcars, and the yards' wooden fences downstream. The river forced the tributary Kansas River into the Argentine and Armourdale neighborhoods, floating more scores of houses downstream.

The river flooded two more times that spring and summer, and it was, in part, our fault. The Missouri River of Lewis and Clark was a wild stream, flowing at its own rhythms and paces. But Americans wanted a predictable river for the modern, industrial era, one we could measure, meter, and subject to cost-benefit analysis. To this end, beginning in 1891 the corps dredged and redirected the river for the benefit of commercial shipping. Over the years, the corps' efforts to build a canal from the Sioux Cities to St. Louis forced the river into an ever smaller channel. The corps operated snag boats that pulled dead trees out of the way. The agency built wood-and-rock structures called wing dikes in the river itself. These narrowed the riverbed and took advantage of the river's power to scour out that channel and keep it clear—the way you might hose out your house gutters. At the same time, all along the river, private landowners, public levee districts, and the corps built thousands of miles of levees.

But we didn't just pay attention to the river itself. Since its creation in 1903, the bureau had been damming the Missouri's tributaries for irrigation projects in the arid West. A dam gathers water from many sources to make a reservoir—streams, springs, snow melt, and storm runoff—and interrupts the ways a river and its tributaries take care of themselves. Although the bureau's dams and reservoirs were the largest, utility companies and many thousands of private landowners throughout the Missouri Basin also built reservoirs and stored water for power generation, livestock, and irrigation. By 1995, federal, state, and local governments, as well as citizens working their lands, had seized the Missouri and its tributaries with over seventeen thousand dams. Since then, we've built another three or four hundred, most of them smaller catch-basin dams at the heads of creeks and streams. When a swollen reservoir overtops a dam, it causes catastrophic failure, and walls of water wash through valleys and down over towns and people once safe from even the worst floods. This means that in flood years like 1943, 1951, 1977, 1993, 1995, and 2011, dam owners and operators flushed their excesses downstream to prevent disaster.

Since nature is anything but predictable, the bureau's dams and the corps' flood-control efforts (channels, dikes, levees, and floodwalls) couldn't always hold back the Missouri. In 1943 the river leaped from its predetermined channel and made its own way. It busted through levees and routed out new channels. It undermined railroad tracks, roads, and bridges.

As a result of the 1943 floods, the bureau and the corps cobbled together two plans — the bureau's centered on irrigation and power generation, while the corps' focused on navigation and flood control. The Flood Control Act of 1944 — also known as the Pick-Sloan Missouri Basin Plan after the agencies' directors — wasn't so much a compromise as the agencies' plans stitched together down the middle. The corps took charge of the Missouri. The bureau controlled the Missouri's tributaries. In total, the plan initially envisioned and built 110 major dams. Of those, 105 backed up tributaries for power and irrigation projects. The other five joined Fort Peck on the Missouri proper, and all of them lay ahead.

It might take months to canoe those waters, and that prospect bothered me. Phone calls and supplies ate away at my meager funds. If I were frugal and encountered no problems, my last $300 would stretch another two months, tops. Before I left Kansas City, I'd paid ahead five months on the rent. It was August now — my fourth month on road and river — and I had six weeks before I'd have to beg my landlord not to evict me. I'd also taken a five-month leave of absence from my job. Any longer and that job would disappear. The thought of seeking another made me tired.

Absence from my daughter, however, weighed on me the most. I could scrabble along the shores of those lakes for months. I might learn to endure the frustration of being stuck on a rock somewhere. Back in Kansas City there were jobs and places to stay. I didn't need to worry about landing on my feet. But I missed my kid.

With the Yellow Pages, my journal, and a good pen, I researched the cost to rent a truck and drive my boat to Yankton, where I'd put in under the last dam on the Missouri and canoe to Kansas City. I called car- and truck-rental companies in Williston, writing down prices in my journal. I weighed the cost against the hardships of canoeing the big lakes. I added my pocket funds and credit card limits, and I calculated how much time went into earning all that back. I hated debt, those strings that bind me to unseen others for periods of servitude. I couldn't analyze benefits in dollars and cents. After an hour, I gave up, agitated and miserable.

So I walked. There is a kind of comfort that comes from being a stranger in a place that's not quite foreign, not quite home. The cover of anonymity helps me escape from myself. Even in the days before the natural gas and oil boom, Williston was a lively place. Two-story storefronts lined Main Street with lots of distractions — shops, restaurants, and bars. It reminded me of towns I'd walked through, such as Marysville, Kansas; North Platte, Nebraska; and Casper, Wyoming. They bound large regions together commercially and socially. It felt good to be out of the motel room and away from myself. After a while, I settled on a bench near a downtown restaurant and watched people for a long time.

As afternoon faded into evening, a woman sat down at my bench and introduced herself. She was tall and wore old-fashioned horn-rimmed glasses. She looked vaguely out of place.

"Doris," she said, holding out her hand. "I'm out for a walk and thought I'd sit down. How are ya?" She had a strong North Dakota accent.

"Good," I lied. "Very good."

"You're visiting, aren't ya?" she said.

"How can you tell?"

"People from Williston never sit on these benches."

"You're from Williston," I laughed. "And you sat on this bench."

"Yeah," she said, "but I never introduce myself to strangers."

As I had walked from Kansas City to Helena, people introduced themselves and started conversations out of the blue a hundred times. But never had anyone looked so . . . out of date. Doris was about fifty. She wore polyester double-knit slacks, an orangey print blouse with a wide collar, and a neck scarf. She carried a kind of handbag we used to call a "clutch." Her black hair rose from her head in a high bouffant wrapped in a pink ribbon.

She asked about my trip and listened attentively, never looking me in the eye but over my shoulder or at my shoes. She was nervous and stiff, as if she were forcing herself to do something that frightened her.

"Fort Peck Lake nearly killed me," I said, after a long pause that made us both uncomfortable. "It was a disaster. A guy offered to take me around the lake, so I took it. I thought I might try to get past all the lakes to Yankton."

"Well, whaddya know," she said. She became animated, and she gesticulated randomly. "I know just the guy to help you out. Why, yes, I know a man, a friend of mine. He goes there all the time. To Yankton, I mean. Oh, all the time. He has a pickup truck. Your canoe will fit in a truck, won't it? Maybe, he'll take you. That would be nice, now wouldn't it?"

"That's all right," I said, "Really. I'm renting a truck." I decided in that second.

"Oh, no, no," she interrupted. "That's just silly. It will cost you a fortune, a real fortune. Nobody has that kind of money. Let's see if my friend has time."

She stood and started down the street.

I walked behind her, feeling self-conscious. Who is this? I thought. Why is she so awkward? So friendly? What does she want? Yankton's 750 miles away. She can't know what she's putting her friend up to. Maybe she's a lunatic.

I'd learned to trust my intuition when it came to strangers. She didn't feel threatening. Sometimes people needed or wanted a charity case. Her friend would say no, I thought, but it would make her feel good to ask.

Doris walked over to a pay phone and dug change from her patent-leather handbag. I paced until she finished her call.

"Let's go see Rick, my friend," she said, coming out of the booth. "He says he can help you."

I almost fell over.

She chattered aimlessly as we drove in her sensible, four-door car over to an apartment complex. Rick sat at a small desk in his cramped studio. He was about fifty, rotund, with a few days' growth on his face. He wore thick glasses.

"Doris told me about your trip and your problem with that big water," he said. "I get it. Once in a while, I'll go out with some friends in a pontoon. That water gets rugged, oh, boy." There were no chairs but the one he was sitting in. He motioned for me to sit on the bed. Doris was in the kitchen making tea and putting ice in glasses, rattling around and whistling as if she lived there and we were her guests.

"I can help you out," he said. "I have to go to Mitchell, South Dakota, to take care of a little business in about a week. I can take you down to Yankton. Whaddya think?"

He looked up at me from his chair. Doris stood still, a glass of iced tea in each hand. They were quiet and anxious.

"Sure," I said.

"Oh, that's fantastic!" Doris said, her voice booming in the tiny apartment. "Just fantastic."

"I was thinking about this trip for a while," Rick said. "You're about as good an excuse as any. But it's a fifteen hundred–mile round trip. Gas and a night in a motel would do it for me. Would you mind?"

Mind? Shit, no.

"Only thing is," he continued. "I take care of some old folks. Keeps me from thinking too much about myself, you know. It'll be a week before we can rip. Think you can put up with Doris that long?"

"Doris?" I said. I didn't know what putting up with her meant.

"Sure," she said. She handed us the glasses and sat down on the other end of the bed from me. "You can sleep in my extra room. I'd love to have ya. Yes. That'll be great."

All of it made me dizzy. Not a day out of the boat and I get a ride into town, a ride to Yankton, and a place to stay while I waited.

"Doris," I said on the way to the motel. "I don't know about all this. I mean, I'm a stranger."

"Oh, come on, now," she said. "You'll be fine."

I met Doris in the lobby the next morning. She was dressed in an orange, red, and yellow polyester pantsuit. She was as tall as I was, and her hair towered above her.

She insisted she buy breakfast for us in the motel restaurant. We took a booth next to the counter where working men sat at stools. The waitresses were filling a long glass case with plates of meringue and cream pies.

"Doris," I said after the waitress took our orders, "I don't want to offend you or anything, but why have you been so quick to help?"

"Well, you see," she said, hesitating. She kept looking down at the table or out the window. She smiled nervously. "I've only been out of the mental hospital for about a month."

Oh, brother, I thought.

"Don't let that scare you," she said. "Really. I wasn't homicidal. Nothing like that." She cackled so loud people turned to see. "After my husband left me, I locked myself up in my house for five years. Five years, can you believe it? I couldn't move at first, you know. Then I got depressed, so I just stayed in. I never left. People brought me all the things I needed — food, cleaning supplies, magazines. Oh, they were so nice. All I did was watch television. I only agreed to a divorce after I ran out of money. Being broke'll do that to ya." She laughed a loud hoot that rang through the diner. "Boy, oh, boy! I wasn't going to give up. But they were going to turn off the water and lights. Winter was coming.

"Don't ask me what I was thinking. I wanted all my husband's money for leaving me. But he probably thought I was losing my mind." She laughed again, turning heads in the diner. "And he was right. He was a saint. He checked on me every day and bought most of my food."

Her husband had paid for everything — the house, the car, and later, the mental hospital. The divorce settlement, she said, put all those things into writing.

"My friends and my ex-husband tried to get me out of the house, you know," she said. "They'd make appointments for me at the beauty parlor or at the doctor. But I never went. They'd invite themselves over. I don't suppose I was good company. After a while, that sort of stopped. There are four years I hardly remember. It was all the same. I kept the curtains pulled, you know, and unplugged all the clocks. I hardly knew when it was day or night.

"Finally, my ex-husband and my friend Evangeline and her husband, Don — that guy's the chief of police! — they got me committed. They thought I was going to drink Drano or something.

"Boy, when the police showed up, it was like more TV. I wanted to get mad, you know. But it was like a TV show about me. The only thing I worried about was being seen in public. So I wrapped my head in a bath towel."

She laughed again in a loud, screeching guffaw. Doris didn't notice that she drew everyone's attention. I couldn't help but laugh myself.

Doris was goofy in the way one gets after being alone for too long. She snorted when she laughed, and she laughed at herself and her own jokes. She slapped me on the arm in a careless, clumsy sort of way. She talked herself through things. "Now, if I look in here, I'll find my car keys. Well, whaddya know? There they are." She smiled all the time, waved to people she didn't know, and said things like, "You know how much a town changes in five years? My God, it's amazing."

I could feel she was still enjoying the smell of fresh air and experiencing a great uplift after her self-imprisonment. She had a spark I found infectious. Meeting me, she said, gave her reason to cook and clean. I suspected she looked forward to the human contact she'd missed for so long.

"I like being out of the house," she said. "Lock yourself up too long and you forget that, you know." Since she'd left the hospital, she tended large flower gardens in the yard of her ranch-style house. She loved to decorate, she said. "Mostly cutesy bric-a-brac. I love shopping for bric-a-brac." She took her car to the car wash once a week, "Whether I've driven it anywhere or not. Those men at the car wash are so nice to me. I'd take it twice a week, but they might figure out what I'm up to."

She laughed and snorted and slapped me on the arm.

For the next week, I slept in the finished bedroom in Doris's basement. The small window didn't let in much light, but the room was clean and cozy. Besides a bed, Doris furnished the room with a small writing table and a couple of lamps. Family pictures hung on the walls and stood in small frames on the desk and chest of drawers.

Mornings, I woke when Doris's footsteps squeaked the floor above. She made breakfast and insisted on making the bed every day. She laundered and folded my clothes. She let me use her phone to call my daughter every afternoon. ("Ha!" she said when I wanted to pay her. "I don't know the last time I paid a long-distance bill. This is so much fun.") We ate out every other day in Williston diners and family restaurants with friends who seemed glad to have Doris back. They came and went at different times of the day, often settling in for long chats.

Afternoons, Doris and I sat on her patio and drank gallons of iced tea and ate bags and bags of potato chips. "Hey," she said more than once. "Whaddya say to some ice cream?"

And I walked. I participated in social life anonymously. Williston had two movie theaters a block from each other on Main Street. I watched all five movies showing that week. Spending time at a coffeehouse and a bookstore not far from the theaters, I ended several days on the park bench where I had met Doris.

When I wasn't distracting myself, I was lost, preoccupied with the river and what I might face on my return home.

Doris prepared a sumptuous dinner for my last night in Williston. She, her sister, and her mother joined Rick and I at the dining room table. Four of her friends were there as well. Doris had cooked all day — pork chops, corn, potatoes, salad, fried-zucchini appetizers, fresh bread, and fresh iced tea and hand-squeezed lemonade.

"You like Williston?" Doris's mother asked. She was seventy and had a healthy energy about her. Unlike Doris, she wore cotton.

"It joins the towns where I'd live on purpose."

"It's quiet, but it's the center of something," she said. "The closest city to here is Minot, eighty miles east. The rest is farmers and miners, the irrigation boys. We have a lot here. Parks and things to see. There's a comfortable movie house . . . You saw a movie this week, I hope."

"Five. And Williston has a good bookshop."

"Don't need much, do ya?" she said with a smile. "That's good. That's refreshing."

"I like it that way," I said.

After everyone left, Doris squeaked around upstairs as I wrote at the table in my room in the basement. The floorboards fell silent after a while. The sounds of the water heater and air conditioner took over. Light from the streetlight in the alley spilled in the small window near the ceiling, making lines of dim blue across the bedspread.

I turned the lights out and lay down in that glow. I wanted to go home but didn't. I missed my kid but liked getting up in the morning whenever it was time, doing whatever I wanted, getting on the river when I wanted, and getting off when I'd had enough. Living in a canoe was a fine life.

Except for Sydney, home was a place that could wait. It would be there. Now I was hopping over weeks of paddling. Maybe that was too quick.

I dreamed of the river, felt the canoe rock back and forth. Cows watched in silence from the top of high, grass-covered banks. River turned into road — the rhythm of walking, the same as that of paddling. I thought I heard the creaking of wagon wheels through dry grass, and I woke to Doris preparing breakfast upstairs.

Rick and I drove down to the U.S. 85 bridge and found the canoe safe where I'd left it. We tied it to the top of his pickup, which had a shell on the bed, and headed south out of Williston on U.S. 85. The road shot flat and straight through the prairies. My mind kept wandering back to the river and what I missed by taking the canoe on the road. We stopped for meals and coffee in roadhouses and truck stops. The vast prairie began to break up, first with rolling hills topped with pine and then the foothills that rose into the pine-carpeted Black Hills. The day was clear and bright, the air cooling as we drove higher.

"Too bad we won't see Mount Rushmore," Rick said.

"Uh, yeah, too bad." I didn't mean to sound unenthused, but it was in my voice.

"Anxious, are ya? Want to get back on the river and get home?"

"I miss the river," I said. "I want to see my daughter, but I'm not sure I want to go home anymore."

While Rick tended to his business in Mitchell, I walked through town in a haze and found myself in front of the Corn Palace, a large auditorium covered from top to bottom with different colors of corn cobs. I remember looking at the Corn Palace and asking myself what attached people to place. Kansas City was my home, but I would never cover a building with corn to show it off.

Rick and I talked. I remember his face and his voice. But today I couldn't tell you what we talked about, except for snippets in my notes. I've searched my journals for more references to the 750 miles from Williston through Rapid City and on to Yankton. All I find is this: "I want to see Sydney, be her father, guide her if I can. I don't want to go home."

I recognize the problem now. It happens every time I take a trip. Being underway intoxicates me. Out from beneath the fog of routine, the stifling sameness of work and home, I see the possibilities in life. Many people vacation and come back refreshed. I travel and return, sorry to be home. I hate going home. But I don't know how it would feel or what I'd do if I couldn't come home.

Skipping the reservoirs from Williston to Yankton really bugged me. I felt like I was giving up, disappointing myself and the people who had supported me on this journey. How would I tell them I would not or could not canoe all that open water in the wind? Would my grave marker, like those in the Fort Buford cemetery, speak of disappointment and failure?

We stopped at a motel outside Yankton. I remember only the brightly lit parking lot and me and Rick dragging ourselves into the room and falling on the beds. Exhausted as I was, I didn't fall asleep until dawn. I felt resentful. People made the river work for them and had taken it from me. They folded it up and put it in a bucket, the bottom of which no one wanted to see.

14 A Startling Leap

GREEN AND TRANSLUCENT WALLS OF WATER SPILLED through all fourteen floodgates above the Gavin's Point Dam concrete floodway. They fell in slow motion, turned white, and met in a great spray of foam and sound on the curving downstream wall of the dam.

The woman at the visitor's center above the dam said the corps decided that morning to release 100,000 cubic feet of water per second from Lewis and Clark Lake. That was an engineer's way of saying "a lot." An amount of water flowing one foot wide, one foot deep at one foot every second doesn't make much sense unless you're in the measuring business. Because of a river's depth, speed, and volume, it's hard for most of us to imagine it as one-foot cubes. To put this in perspective, one cubic foot means seven and a half gallons per second, or 449 gallons per minute — enough water to fill a six-person hot tub. The flow over the dam that day represented a little less than an Olympic-sized swimming pool every second or fifty-two of them every minute. In 1995 the releases from Lewis and Clark Lake eclipsed those of 1993. The lake hadn't been as full since the 1977 Missouri River floods and would not be again until 2011. In 2011 the corps let out of the lake 150,000 cubic feet per second — seventy-eight swimming pools every second — to keep the reservoir from running around the sides of the dam and causing it all to collapse.

Numbers made no sense here. In 1995 the Missouri roared over that dam with the snarl and laughter of a wild creature demonstrating its power to the puny beings who sought to control it. I felt drawn into that incomprehensible mass of rushing river — the same feeling I get standing next to a speeding train or peeking over the rim of the Grand Canyon. I loved it and wanted to climb over the rail and jump into the flume as if it were a water park slide. Leaning out over the water racing past me, I screamed and yelled but couldn't hear myself.

At midmorning I canoed away from the campground. Past the dam's spillway and out into the valley, the Missouri slowed and soon spread out like a moving lake. This was not the river of the semiarid Montana and North Dakota plains but of the verdant Midwest. The air was thick as a woolen blanket drenched in warm water. The river here was greener, milkier than when I left it eight hundred miles upstream. The landscape of jagged edges and abrupt drop-offs so prominent above Lake Saka-kawea had disappeared. The banks rolled to the river in gradual slopes. Behind the levees, the landscape was deeply, lushly green, almost like jungle compared to the sagebrushy West. Cottonwood, ash, sycamore, and elm grew up from tangles of horsetail reeds, grapevines, and Virginia creeper. The big leaves of pokeweed waved in the breeze. Wide valleys separated long, tree-blanketed hills. The air smelled like grocery-store vegetables mixed with honey and roses, green odors I associated with goldenrod, ragweed, and honeysuckle. All of it felt the way the first thunderstorm of spring feels, familiar but strange and new.

Since Wolf Creek, each morning had been the start of a private conversation between the Missouri and me. The river's mood and cir-cumstance changed over the course of a day, much the way mine might between breakfast and dinner, though I remained the same person. The Missouri was reliable in its steady, determined drive to the sea. Going around Fort Peck Lake I wound up on a river of similar size and in com-parable landscape to that which I had left. Leaving the river in Williston and arriving back to it eight hundred miles downstream, however, was like meeting a person I had not seen in years. The face was familiar, as was the voice and manner of speaking. But we had taken different paths and had experienced different things since we last talked. Our conversa-tion would be much different from now on.

At Yankton my journey bumped into a kind of mental sandbar just four miles from the dam. A number of contradictions that had plagued me for some time piled up on one another in the short distance between Gavins Point and Yankton's riverfront park: I wanted to get home to my daughter and my friends, but I didn't look forward to returning. I never wanted to leave the river. I knew I had changed, and the people and culture of my city had not. I couldn't stand the thought of the disappointment and discontent that happens to me when I return home from a long trip. I wanted a clean bed and hot shower but loved the lack of them more. Their absence meant freedom from material goods, jobs, and grinding routines. I wanted to live on the river, but other people depended on me. If I wanted to be a father, I had to go home.

Fortunately, though I'd never been to Yankton, an old pal of mine lived there. I tied the canoe to a dock at the town's riverfront park and used a pay phone. My friend was getting ready for vacation. We had not talked in months and had a good, if too-short, conversation. He said a friend of his had arrived in town for a family visit but was already itching for a break. He called his friend to tell him who I was and where I'd be. We would, he said, get on famously.

I sat on the dock that was not much more than a floating wood-plank walk. The river rose and fell gently. I felt danger that I could not identify. Though all my common sense and rational mind told me otherwise, I felt as if there were sea monsters under the water or gunmen in the trees.

My intuition told me to stay ashore. The riverfront park was as good a place as any for an overnight. I'd let the anxiety pass and then start downstream. Evenly spaced "No Camping" signs stood up and down the waterfront. I'd sleep under the stars and handle the cops when the time came.

Decision made, I stared out at the river. The dread abated.

Soon a healthy-looking man named Todd Christensen tromped across the dock toward me. He asked if I was the guy traveling to Kansas City.

"How are you?" he said, sitting down next to me. The river swirled around the canoe, making little eddies. The scene was calm, serene. Cars bumped over the old steel bridge just upstream, and sounds of the town filtered down through the wind.

"Good," I said. I was, to him, a stranger. I supposed I could tell him anything. Even lies. But I wasn't willing, so I just told him the truth.

"No, I'm sorry," I said. "Not good and not bad. It's a funny thing. I'm ready to go home, but I don't want to face what I might find there. I like it out here. There's nothing and everything to do. It's boring as shit, and it's exciting as anything I've ever done. I would love to visit home the way you and I are visiting now. But I don't want to stay there."

"Woo-hoo," he said, rolling his eyes. "I know what you're going through. I've traveled quite a bit. Not only for business or vacation but just because. The kind of feelings you describe scare the crap out of me. It's pure confusion, and I hate it."

"I miss my daughter," I said. "I don't miss home and the life I live there."

"Kansas City, right?"

"Yes," I said. "It means a job, a house, you know, a regular life. No more of this Huck Finn stuff. I want to visit, I suppose, get ready for winter, and take the river to Saint Louis and on to the Gulf. Then I'd go someplace else and start over again. As soon as I say that, though, I think of something that contradicts it. Mostly, all of it makes me want to disappear."

"It sounds like you're afraid of going home and finding out how much you've changed and how much it hasn't," he said. "You can't go home again, you know, not because it's a strange place but because you've become a stranger."

"Worse," I said. "A stranger in a familiar place."

"Well, now that that's out of the way. Let's quit moping."

After checking my knots on the canoe and dock, we drove into Yankton, a small, pretty town with clean streets and old houses. Although forty-five, Todd looked ten years younger. His blond hair flopped around in the wind through the car window. A painter who had shown his work at galleries and exhibitions, he also worked as a freelance illustrator. Occasionally he did back-scenes production for Hollywood movies. He lived with his girlfriend on the beach in Venice, California, and had come to Yankton for a family reunion.

As we drove, he pointed out places and told stories of his youth associated with them. He looked back through time and sounded like many other people I'd met on this journey. He told of his experience without the input, mediation, or contradiction of others who may have seen things differently. He acted as if he had always known me, but not with the strained and overly friendly familiarity of someone starved for attention. He seemed, rather, a kindred spirit. In pursuit of a creative career, he left his small midwestern town far behind. He had traveled, seen new places, and experienced new ways of life. He understood the ways these things altered him far more clearly than I could perceive the same kinds of changes in myself.

His parents, Pat and Pal Christensen, were sitting in lawn chairs on their porch when we arrived. Todd introduced us and briefly told them about my trip. They nodded their heads in approval. He told them I was staying the night. They approved of that too.

Like Todd, his parents looked young for their ages. They were in their sixties. Pat was open and friendly, a strong woman with a lovely glow in her face. Pal was robust and energetic, a retired salesman. They had raised nine kids. Pal provided, he said, "when being a salesman was good." He still did some business in Kansas City. But he said, "I wouldn't want to start selling anything now. The competition was always rough. Today it's murder. I'm glad I'm out of it. I wouldn't wish it on any of my kids."

Willy Loman, he wasn't.

He tipped his glass toward what looked to be a college campus across the street. Hedges and tall oaks surrounded august brick buildings. Below, a low wrought-iron fence outlined an immaculately manicured lawn. Men dressed in polo shirts and shorts walked along the sidewalks. A few played tennis at courts beneath the trees.

"It used to be Yankton College," Pat said, picking up where Pal's gesture left off. "It's a federal prison, you know. One of those white-collar prisons. There're no fences except that little one around the place, no walls."

"See those guys at the doors?" Pal said.

Two official-looking men stood at the entrances to each of the buildings.

"Prison guards," he said. "Every one of them. And those guys walking and playing tennis over there? Prisoners. They take one step off the sidewalk or chase a tennis ball across the yard and they get written up. Three violations and they're sent to Leavenworth.

"Quiet place, real quiet," he continued. "Eight hundred criminals.

Big cheeses serve their time over there. Lots of them are smart guys, people who made fortunes or who tried the wrong way. They'll get out and go make more. They probably have a few mobsters over there, too."

Yankton College was 103 years old when it closed in 1984. Its conversion to a prison in 1988 was a good thing for Yankton, Pal said, as well as for his neighborhood. Yankton College used to be a good school, with high standards and quality students.

"But toward the end, yee-haw!" he said, rolling his eyes. "They were desperate and let just about anyone in there."

"The clientele's better now," Pat said. "And the campus is better kept than when it was the college."

Todd and I spent the next two days together. We took long drives and talked. When he came home for visits, he usually stayed close to his family's house, except to drive to his brother's farm in the country. But now he took me places he had avoided or not seen in years. Clapboard houses lined the streets of Yankton side by side with trim three-story Victorians. Oaks and walnuts broadcast cool shade on the ground below them. He told stories about what happened or what he had done in an alley, on a corner, or along a street. We drove out of town and into a Midwest we had in common. Hardwood forest grew on the hills and valleys between fields of row crops and cow pastures. Honeysuckle, grapevines, and trumpet vines climbed telephone poles and up the sides of barns and tool sheds. In the evening, I left Todd and his family and walked past the college and back out to the west edge of town to watch the sunset. Paved roads ran off into rows of corn and fields of beans. Telephone and electrical wires laced the landscape. Farmhouses studded the fields and hills to the horizon.

I told Todd about this feeling of familiarity with the landscape and the comfort I felt in it.

"I visit home every year or so," he said. We sat on the porch in Pal's and Pat's chairs. All the inmates had gone inside, and the prison campus was quiet. Nighthawks called in the open spaces, and bats fluttered between the trees along the street.

"Somehow, the place doesn't change. I love it, the people, the land. It's good to get away from the ocean. But I could never come back here for long. It just isn't 'home' anymore," he said, raising his fingers to signal air quotes. "I hope Kansas City isn't like that for you."

"Even if it is," I said, "I have a reason to stay. My daughter Sydney's just a kid, and her mom lives there. I won't take her away from her mother. Her mom's not leaving Kansas City. She's not the type."

"Then I hope this trip makes staying on easier."

"The good thing," I said, "is that life won't be the same. I don't know what it'll be yet. I won't get back into the miserable rut I was in before I left. If the trip's showed me anything, it's that."

My last night in Yankton, we drove out to his brother's farm for dinner, a big affair in the kitchen of a neat, renovated farmhouse. John, Todd's younger brother, was a wiry, tall man with dark eyes and a sunny disposition. After dinner the three of us drove in John's pickup to a small lake down the road and listened to the coyotes. The sun had set, and the first stars had popped into the night. The air was cool, and the breeze gentle.

"I love it here," Todd said.

"I don't really know much else," John said. "But land is like that. You know it, and you never really know it. You become a part of it, and it becomes you. But it's still separate. It sort of has its own life you can't control. You're familiar with it, but there's always stuff you've never seen."

I've never heard a better description of the Missouri River.

Todd, Pal, and I set the canoe on the river the next day at the dock.

"It's all easy from here," Todd said. "You'll be home in no time."

The sky was clear. A breeze washed the river's fishy-green fug over us. I stepped into the canoe. The fear I had felt just a few days before had disappeared. Home was still over four hundred miles and a couple of weeks away. I didn't have to try to sort out all the conflicts now. Todd showed me that. Things would become clear if I let them. The well-worn AA phrase, "One day at time," was becoming more meaningful to me.

Downstream from Yankton the river widened and flowed through numerous channels and over sandbars. The water had risen to the point that it lapped against levees. Rain clouds formed near the horizon and soon covered the sky.

Near Vermillion a whole neighborhood of flood-stained houses hung in crazy angles in the branches of the cottonwoods along the banks. Open front doors swung twenty feet above the water. Below, the river had piled all sorts of outbuildings, boats, boat trailers, and store signs against the trees. Most of the buildings folded over one direction or the other, and many were upside down or on their sides. The boats and cars stuck out of heaps of driftwood and sometimes astride them. Dried swatches of algae swathed many of these buildings and sheds and boats and cars. Dirty watermarks ran parallel with the river across it all.

The river flowed lovely and strong beneath a great deal of suffering. I thought of the difference between flood and high water. High water was a condition of weather and topography. Cottonwoods evolved in river basins and depended on high water for their propagation. Such events, at the same time, scoured the brush from beneath the cottonwoods and made room for deer, coyotes, raccoons, and birds. But floods occurred wherever humans and rivers interacted. Building lives and assets on the river's property made some people a lot of money and produced misery for many others. Transportation and trade brought us to the river. The power of our machines allowed us to believe we controlled the river or could control it. In the flush of success, we built more levees and channeled more riverbed and turned more water into money. Holding back high water, we felt safe and built more assets, lives, and livelihoods in the floodplain. Then in years such as 1977, 1993, 1995, and 2011, the river showed who was in charge.

Anything we put in the river bottom was at risk, and avoiding flood came as easily as building on higher ground. Something as sensible as choosing a different location would have made the damming of the Missouri and the building of Fort Peck Lake and all the reservoirs unnecessary.

But life was never that simple. People didn't build in a floodplain to have the Missouri wash their houses away. They built there because it was easy and made sense at the time. I passed those piles of metal, lumber, and plastic and saw the hopes and dreams of someone like me there. Each wrecked house or car represented a piece of someone's life.

At sunset near Burbank—a tiny town of two streets one way and three the other—the sky darkened and the wind kicked up to a roar, heavy with the smell of rain. I pulled my boat up to an island in the middle of the river, an old sandbar where a few cottonwoods and willows had taken root. It seemed a great place to overnight. But no part on the island rose more than a foot above the river. New releases from Gavins Point Dam would raise the river, likely inundating the island.

The storm built quickly, however. The sky turned black, laced with tiny cracks of sunset orange. Within a minute or two, the wind blew waves upstream and soon formed them into angry and rolling walls of water over two feet high. I pulled the boat back up on the island as far as I could. I tied off to a tree and set the tent. I barely zipped it closed before the rain and hail hit. The wind bowed the canvas onto my back. Through the roar of hail came a sound similar to jet engines in the clouds above, as if B-52s were flying in to land on Burbank's main street.

I could feel rain draining off of and running under the tent. I imagined the river would begin flowing over the island. If that happened, I was helpless. I wondered if I would get home. Then I began to ask myself if I would be able to stay at home if I got there. I put my head on my makeshift pillow of T-shirts and listened to that storm. It pulsed and whirred, the sounds of wind, rain, and hail winding around like a great machine. I thought I might never hear anything like it again.

A thousand pats and swishes against the tent canvas woke me in the night. The sounds puzzled me as I wondered what forest or river animal made this noise: lizards, snakes, bugs and beetles, beavers, minks, otters? Nothing made sense. Raccoons and skunks were hardly subtle, pat-patting creatures. Deer wouldn't come near a tent.

I had to see. I rose quietly from my sleeping bag. Unzipping the door a crack, I pushed out the flashlight and shined it on the ground in front of the tent.

I think I felt my eyes bug out of my head. Where there was supposed to be sand, a shifting pool of yellow specks beamed back at me. Some of those little eyes jumped. I opened the tent more to get a closer look. As I did, a sea of frogs squeaked and whined. Soon the sound gathered into a collective high-pitched whistle so loud it hurt my ears. I turned off my light, and their voices faded. I turned it on again, and they wailed in response. After I zipped the tent shut and switched off the lamp, the pats against the tent continued. Heavy rain had driven the frogs from beneath the sand and out of the leaf litter and the grass on the island. Attracted to the heat of my body, they jumped randomly over one another in a moving carpet, those along the closest edge leaping up against the nylon and sliding back down.

What a savagely beautiful day. I closed my eyes and saw again the orange glow of the sunset shining through the storm, the ocean of frogs, and the waves moving upstream. The thunder, the storm, and the frogs whistling in the night had been so loud. Now there was nothing but the soft pat and swish of frogs hopping up against the canvas and sliding back to the ground.

The frogs had disappeared by morning. When I climbed out of my tent, I looked closely at the ground. No evidence of them remained in the sand.

Maybe, I thought, I had been dreaming. Even today I wonder.

15 Rather Be Fishing

THE RIVER GOT MUDDIER AS MY THOUGHTS GREW CLEARER. At Wolf Creek, imaginary tree branches, snags, and whirlpools had frightened me the most. With experience, I no longer feared such things or the river itself. Rapids, thunderstorms, and tornadoes and waterspouts hadn't killed me. I had come over three thousand miles from my porch and was just four hundred river miles from returning to it. Over that distance, I found I dread the process of maturing. Neither the river nor its twists and turns could cure such affliction. They could only show me my insides and make me wrestle with growing self-awareness. And there is no work I like less than that which leads me to know myself.

Facing challenges, proving my mettle, and gaining physical strength sound like fantastic goals. But they are abstract and, in the end, more easily met than understanding how to be an adult. Damn the Missouri River.

After Burbank I floated into a long stretch of sandbars, easy bends, and braided stream. In the distance thick hardwood forest blanketed the rolling hills. Vast farms covered the bottoms below. A few trailers and cabins stood on stilts behind isolated stands of cottonwoods.

The day started with that heavy humidity I so love and hate about the Midwest. You break a sweat just getting out of bed. Without even trying, I was sopping wet by the time I got into the boat. After the sun rose above the trees, everything in the boat from my bags to the gunwales and the paddle was burning, roasting hot. By midmorning the steamy air caught in my chest and made every move seem like real work. The day even sounded hot. Crickets sawed in the grass, and the last of the summer cicadas buzzed in the trees. The river itself gave no relief.

I dawdled. These would be my last bits of isolation on the river. Past the Sioux Cities, the river flows through sprawling metropolitan areas like Omaha, Nebraska; Council Bluffs, Iowa; and St. Joseph, Missouri. I'd float twenty-five miles through a city like Omaha, for instance; but only three or four miles would be urban and the rest, suburbs, exurbs, and outlying industrial parks. Once the noise began, it would be expressways and air conditioners, cement plants and grain elevators, and motorboats and bad music all the way home.

So I jacked around. The boat didn't need me. It moved by itself on water flat and smooth as glass. I read and caught up on my journal. I baked and took long naps in the sun.

In high summer this stretch of the Missouri courses as fat and warm as sidewalk puddles in the sun. The National Park Service maintains free-flowing stretches of the Missouri above and below Lewis and Clark Lake called the Missouri National Recreation River. One of those stretches runs from Gavins Point Dam almost to the Sioux Cities, about sixty miles; the other runs forty miles upstream of the lake. These hundred miles are two-thirds of the river left that Americans do not dredge, channel, dam, or dike. The other remaining length of free-running river flows between Lake Sakakawea and Lake Oahe through Bismarck, North Dakota.

"Free-flowing" does not mean pristine, untouched, or unfettered. I had an island to camp on near Burbank precisely because the river does not flow uninhibited. Over the past 150 years, we have altered all but the first miles of the Missouri. With the heavy touch of human hands, the river no longer wears down its banks or moves its sandbars the same way it did two centuries ago. The big dams upstream from Gavins Point and the seventeen-thousand-plus smaller private and government dams in the basin control the flow of the river, some of it even before it becomes the Missouri at the Three Forks. Because of these dams, the river does not meander in wet seasons anymore. Even if it leaves its banks, long levees prevent it from going far. In Montana, cows and sheep graze land next to the river. They leave some grass, willows, and trees so that one could, with effort, maintain the illusion of unspoiled nature. After Yankton, however, corn grew on the river's banks.

Leaving the river in North Dakota, I arrived in my green-tangled Midwest having missed all seven hundred miles of transitions and subtleties in landscape and climate. The river lived its own life for hundreds of miles while I was away for only a week or so. These things happen. When I fly, I sit down in a big room in one place and get out a couple of hours or half a day later in other lands, climates, and landscapes. After Burbank I recognized the river as the one of my youth. It made me miss the stretches of river I skipped all the more.

I floated most of the morning and into the afternoon through the last twelve miles of the National Recreation River. At Ponca, Nebraska, the Missouri began a fierce struggle against a further change in human commands. It coursed past a great wooded bluff. There, an even bed of gray limestone rubble called revetment took the place of cars and building debris that farmers upstream used to keep the river out of their land. The Corps of Engineers had driven thousands of cypress logs into the banks that kept the limestone in place. Rock dikes and jetties constricted the river further and made sweeping arcs out of tight curves.

Within just a few miles, the Missouri — which had been a mile or more broad above Ponca — narrowed to less than six or seven hundred feet. The Missouri fought its new confines and reverberated against its limestone banks. It speeded up. Swells formed even, rounded stair steps on the river. Boils burst up from the depths and spread across the river's surface. As it bowled around curves, the river eddied and belched and churned. It turned from translucent green to muddy brown. The land shifted from stark tree-empty farmland to hills heavy with rich vegetation. This was the river I knew, where lusty, full grapevines, stands of reeds, and willows lolled in the water. The air smelled green and fishy, laced with honeysuckle. It was paradise.

I paddled between those dark-green banks into flotillas of boats of all sizes and shapes. Jet Skis raced by. Powerful motorboats pulled smiling water skiers. The wakes trapped in the narrow channel churned up the water. Standing waves crashed over my bow. My canoe was the only one on the river. Remembering the tough time I had at Great Falls, I saw how I'd gained skill since. I had fun sloshing up and down among the motorboats. I sang to myself.

One boat rumbled upstream past me, and its engines stopped. The young couple at the helm took to the back seat and popped open a couple of cans of beer. The woman pulled a glass water pipe from a storage bin and bent over it. I laughed. It had been at least a decade since I'd smoked any weed, and I hated it even then. But I loved stoners. A few rounds of a water pipe or joint allowed them to think almost everything they said or did was funny. Their mirth made me laugh. As the boat drifted out of the current to the side, the man stood and started the engine. He steered the boat back to the center of the channel and sat back down again.

We drifted closer together. The man invited me to come alongside. I gripped a chrome handle on his boat and bobbed along.

"Why don't you tie up and step in?" he said. "We're just drifting."

I took a seat and thanked them. They introduced themselves as Paul and Shawna. They were in their late twenties. Paul had dark hair and blue eyes. He wore swim trunks. His rippled chest and stomach were bare. Shawna wore a bikini, her blond hair brushing her shoulders. He was a bond trader; she, an interior designer. They beamed the freshness of youth.

"Great boat, eh?" he said. It was a powerful fiberglass and vinyl craft with seats for seven or eight people.

"Fine boat," I said. "What are all these people doing out here? I mean, some are skiing, but everyone else is just sitting around."

"Weed?" he held out the short glass water pipe.

"No, thanks," I said. "You don't have enough potato chips for me to get started."

"Too bad," he said, lighting up. "They're just drifting like we are. We put in at South Sioux City and come upstream, then just float all the way back to town."

I loved the way he spoke while holding his breath.

Drifting downstream, it turns out, is a grand pastime for people in South Sioux City, Nebraska, and Sioux City, Iowa. At Kansas City only a few anglers used the river. Here it was like a carnival. Like other boaters, Paul and Shawna sat back and soaked up sun. Without exception, I could see the other drifters bobbing around in their boats drinking beer, lots of beer. Remembering those lost afternoons that turned into hungover mornings, I'm glad I wasn't drinking and didn't want to.

"When there's no one else around, we can get a little intimate,"

Shawna said with a smile more innocent and open than lascivious. "But today's too busy. Besides, how often do you find someone on the river with a canoe?"

"This is the first time," Paul said in answer. "We're out here a lot. Just about every weekend. We've never seen a canoe.

"We live in South Sioux City. We have a little place out by the highway. It's not big or anything, just nice. Both of us have good jobs, so we decided last year to get us a boat. Kinda expensive but it's fun. It's nice to come out here when it's hot and just cool out in the sun."

They looked pretty cooled out. We drifted the next ten miles, talking. Once in a while, Shawna fetched new rounds of beer from a cooler under one of the seats. Between bong hits, they shared cigarettes. They revealed too much about themselves; and being an eavesdropper and snoop by nature, I listened. According to them, their lives were good and prosperous. They hated the Republican Party; the government of South Sioux City, Iowa; and their neighbor's dog. They loved each other, the river, and making love in the boat when no one was around. They went to church but only reluctantly. A neighbor of theirs fetched the newspaper every day in his underwear, and the woman across the street had a penchant for exposing herself through the bay window.

I liked them a lot.

The motorboat was marvelous, but I noticed how its accommodations detached me from the river. For over two months my view of the world had been three or four feet above the water—the height of the canoe seat above the waterline plus the length of my back. The motorboat gave me an entirely new perspective on the river. Standing up in Paul and Shawna's boat put my eyes seven or more feet above the water. Compared to my canoe, their boat rode solid and steady, rocklike. When I first sat down with them, I braced myself against waves I saw but never felt. In the canoe, I could always feel the river's grip. The wind pushed my boat back and forth, and the waves pulled it side to side. I steered the powerful motorboat once at Paul's invitation. I couldn't feel the river in the wheel.

I much preferred traveling in the canoe, where, at least, the paddle put the river in my hands.

The deep yellow of late evening settled on us by the time we arrived at South Sioux City, Nebraska, across the river from Sioux City, Iowa. They waved as they motored toward the public boat ramp. I pulled my canoe into a small harbor amid dozens of motorboats. Picnickers filled the park. Lines of trucks and cars with trailers pulled boats out of the river at a long concrete ramp. People sat along the grassy bank, watching the river and its traffic. Two men lay sunburned and passed out on the grass near a boat. I could almost feel the heat radiate off them. In the water, six other people pulled and heaved the men's boat onto a trailer by hand. Other companions heaved the drunks into the back of the truck like so much carpet or lumber.

After dark the reflection of a Sioux City riverboat casino on the far bank danced on the water. Lines of casually dressed people filed into the masses of flashing lights, while others walked out in scattered groups. A gentle and cool breeze floated over the water and up over the bank.

I set my tent between neat rows of RVs, where I was an anonymous nobody. Traffic moved along roads on either bank, boats with white and red and green lights spun up and down between the two Sioux Cities. The stars, once as delicate and palpable as a dancer's veils, barely shined in the night sky's bluish urban glow. Below, tangles of Japanese lanterns and Christmas lights hung from camper awnings; the tinny blare of television floated out of lighted windows. Air conditioners on the RVs hummed. Dishes clattered, radios played, and people talked. Someone turned up a stereo and a man howled into the night. Somewhere a hammer pounded metal. These very real human sights and sounds comforted me. I felt contented.

Looking into the lights on the water, watching them bob and tilt and sway, I kept thinking of the cover of Lawrence Ferlinghetti's book of poems *A Coney Island of the Mind*. In the picture, the brightly lit towers of early-twentieth-century Coney Island rise into the night sky. I'd never been to Coney Island, but I imagined it looked something like the Sioux Cities reflected in the Missouri River. I fell asleep listening to the campground, thinking how strange and random human sounds can be. I could feel the river out there, dressed in its cities. I wondered if other people felt the artery of the continent out there. If they did, then this wasn't another of my quirks. If they didn't, maybe they weren't paying attention.

The next day, about thirty miles south of the Sioux Cities at Decatur, two muscled and tanned men on Jet Skis powered away from a tidy riverfront park and up to my canoe. They looked like brothers, one with blond hair and the other with brown.

"You havin' fun out here?" said the blond. "Where ya goin'?"

"Yeah, it's good," I said. "I'm going to Kansas City."

"No shit," said the one with brown hair. "We met another guy out here a couple a days ago on his way to St. Louis. Man, he was havin' a miserable time. He said there's these big lakes up in Montana, and they just about killed him. He rode around them with a friend of his from, I think, just at the beginnin' of that big one . . . what's it called?"

"Fort Pete or something," said the blond.

"Fort Peck, maybe?" I said.

"Yeah, that's right, Fort Pack," said the brown-haired man. "He put in back at Yankton and was comin' down. Said the flood kep' him from findin' arrowheads and fossils on sandbars like he wanted. There ain't a sandbar anywhere. All underwater. Poor guy. Maybe you'll run into him. He's prolly to Omaha by now."

A few miles down from the Jet Skiers, a Nebraska Game and Parks agent in a rig bigger than Paul and Shawna's steered his powerful boat up to me. He had raced up and down the river all day, stopping young kids on Jet Skis, checking anglers' fishing licenses, and chatting with boaters.

"Let me give you a ride," he said.

"You're kidding."

"Nope," he said. "I've watched you paddling along since this morning. I have to go down to Blair and wouldn't mind some company."

I handed my bags up to him, and we pulled the gear into the powerboat and set the canoe in it lengthwise between the seats. He pulled back the throttle, and the boat rose until it glided just on the surface of the water. We stood behind the boat's console and its tiny windshields. He was in his forties, medium height, broad shouldered, and trim. His name was Jon Reeves. He had clear, ice-blue eyes and wore a trim, khaki short-sleeve shirt and pressed pants. Pulling off his green ball cap, he ran his fingers through thinning blond hair. He smiled. His straight teeth seemed all the more white against his tanned skin.

"This has been my job for seventeen years," he said loudly over the wind. "It's a great job. I was in the service and had a couple of other jobs. But after this I don't think I could do anything else. There's only one conservation agent per county, ninety-three of us, and Burt County's mine."

"You don't stay on the river all the time, then?" I said.

"No, but I'm on a lot in the summer, with all the recreational boaters and anglers out. Winter's another thing, deer and turkey season. Plus, running after poachers is still quite a job. Mostly deer, but they're into other stuff, too."

We zipped over the water. The river raced by and seemed faraway. I liked being with Jon but wished I had kept canoeing at my own pace. I wanted to get home but not this quickly.

"I put in and take out at Wilson Island State Park," he said after a few minutes. "That's on the Iowa side. But it's more convenient. The river there can get pretty busy. But most of the traffic is up here, south of Sioux City, so this is where I do most of my work."

Jon wore an automatic pistol in a holster on his hip.

"Ever have any problems?" I said.

"I never had to shoot anybody, yet, if that's what you mean," he said. "I have plenty of minor problems, though. It's rarely more exciting, thank God, than scolding parents of kids on Jet Skis . . . like this bunch."

He powered down, and the boat eased up to a group of three kids in the water. He hailed the Jet Skiers, none of whom were over eleven years old. Mom and Dad sat on lawn chairs on the bank.

"You kids pull over to the bank and get off those Jet Skis," he said. "Don't let me find you back out here." He pulled the boat over toward Mom and Dad. "The kids need to be fourteen or better to be on the water on those things. I'd appreciate it if you would keep them off. The fine's stiff; and if one of the kids gets hurt, then you're in real trouble. Let's not let that happen."

Youch, I thought.

After the kids were into shore, Jon pulled the throttle back, making a sharp turn to head downstream again.

"People don't know sometimes," he said. The boat was moving so fast he was yelling. "They get those things and think they're toys. But they aren't. You get killed just as quick as if you had a boat wreck. The river's no picnic when you're out there and just a little kid. It'll ruin your day — and your parents' day."

He eased back on the throttle, which quieted the wind and allowed him to talk without screaming.

"That kind of thing is what I'm usually after on the river," he continued. "It's the biggest frustration of the job, really. I have a lot to do with wildlife and hunting and fishing, but part of the job is to make sure people have a good time. They get achy when I have to get rough. But in the end, it's just common sense. You don't get drunk and drive a boat. You don't let kids drive the boat. You don't fish or hunt more than your fair share. You don't throw your trash or chemicals in the water. And you don't smoke dope where the ranger can see you."

"You could have written them a ticket?"

"The parents?" he said. "You bet. But why? If I catch them at it again, they'll get a ticket. But probably they won't do it again, at least today. And there's no amount of tickets that will stop them from thinking they can get away with it someplace else."

"Do you ever write tickets?"

"All the time," he said. "Mostly for operating under the influence, fishing without a license, that sort of thing. But I give out tickets to parents who don't think I mean business. Mostly, though, people are pretty good. Poachers get mean and dangerous. They have guns, and when you stop them, you're getting into what they see as their money. But I call on the sheriff when I have to deal with poachers. I never go into that alone."

"Do you ever have to ticket someone in a canoe?" I said.

"Never."

Gliding between the orange and green buoys that marked the navigation channel, we covered forty miles in an hour. Wilson Island State

Recreation Area stood on a peninsula where the river wound tightly back on itself. Trim meadows spread below towering cottonwoods. Beyond the neatly mown grass, tangles of grapevines climbed into the canopy like snakes from thorny tangles of raspberry and rose. The sky darkened and gave the place the feel of a cathedral. The river sloshed around picnic tables and on the road. Grass swayed in the waves like stringy green hair. Minnows splashed in quicksilver streaks under a sky that wanted to dump more rain into the swollen river. Jon pulled his truck up from the boat ramp, trailer and boat spilling water over the concrete.

"If you're ever up this way again," he said, "you know where to find me. It'll be a pleasure to take you for another ride."

When Jon was gone, I was alone in the park. Small weekend cabins stood under the canopy. A row of pop machines hummed at the locked concession stand. At dusk yellow sodium lamps popped on. Beyond the light, the river muscled by silently.

The next day, the sky was low, ominous. Rock quarries, cement plants, refineries, and grain processors on the far side of the Nebraska-side levee thundered with metallic concussions. Along the bank, grapevines tangled cranes, rusting platforms, and dilapidated loading facilities. Moorings, metal, and concrete-filled cylinders called dolphins were skewed in odd angles before the bank. Private boat ramps poked out into the river from eroded dirt roads. People fishing or just watching the river in groups of two and three sat on the bank in lawn chairs next to coolers. Occasionally, trophy homes stood on the bluffs above the river, swaths of bare ground cut in the forest before them to insure a view.

The river flowed straight and fast to the Coast Guard and Corps of Engineers stations north of Omaha—two boat ramps and some metal buildings. Red and green buoys stood in rows on a large concrete platform.

I wanted to find out about these big boats and barges I'd seen as a kid. I didn't know if it would be safe to be in the river with them. I beached my boat and walked up to the Coast Guard station as the sky cleared and humidity rose and drenched the air. Ed Kowalski, a tall, blond-headed man in a neat uniform, got up from a couch in front of a television and let me in the door. Cool, air-conditioned air flowed over us. Kowalski was by himself in the station—keeping watch, he said. His shipmates were out on the *Cheyenne*, a buoy tender that maintained the river channel markers for boaters and shippers.

We played a game of pool in the recreation room of the small quarters, which consisted of a dorm and an office. He poked at a computer after our game and printed out a list of boats expected on the river. Kowalski ripped the computer printout from the printer.

"Two," he said. "You have just two barge packets you might run into this month between here and Kansas City. But for the next few days, the corps has restricted traffic downstream of Kansas City to protect levees. After that, the shipping companies might decide not to run their boats if the commodities or market prices aren't right."

He looked at me seriously for a moment.

"If you come across one of these barge packets, you're gonna be fine," he said. "Just don't be a knucklehead, you know. Leave the channel and be ready to get out. When these boats move downstream, they just make big waves. But when they go upstream, they tear up the water pretty bad. Just watch it. You shouldn't have any problem."

"Is there much traffic on the river when it's not flooded?" I said.

"Nope," he said. "Maybe a boat or two in a summer. Nothing else."

"Is it worth it, you think?" I said. "I mean to maintain a boat channel, buoys, this station?"

"Dude," he said. "I'm a coastguardsman. That's a question I don't ask and a world I can't change. What I really think is that I'd rather be fishing."

16 The Toughest Part

AFTER LEAVING THE COAST GUARD HARBOR, I WAS ALL alone. Despite the city sounds and the life implied in them, nothing in sight moved except the river and the cars on a highway bridge. Neat concrete walking paths wound along the river with no one on them. The air throbbed with the sounds of trucks, trains, and cars. The sharp smells of asphalt and water treatment plants drifted down over the river. Giant storage tanks, truck docks, and metal buildings lined the bank. The buildings at the water plant were eerily empty. On the opposite bank, the Iowa side, farm fields spread out from behind levees and long lines of trees.

The Missouri curved around Omaha's airport, Eppley Airfield, in a half circle. Landing jet planes flew in low and disappeared behind the giant levee and floodwall that kept the river out of the runways and terminal. The roar of departing jets preceded their appearances. As they made the steep climb out of the river valley, engine noise boomed into the river's confinements. The din thrilled me even as it pained my ears and shook my chest. I yelled and whooped. I stood in the boat and screamed over the sound. Not hearing myself when the jet noise was loudest, I screamed all the louder.

Coming out of the big curve in the river near the airport, I entered urban Omaha. Like a beached whale, a submarine lolled on the bank a mile or so ahead. Heat, I thought. Sunstroke. I stood again in the boat to get a better look.

Wonders, I thought, as I floated toward the submarine. The Missouri River was one after another.

Just before the submarine, a bay opened on the Omaha bank. Empty boat slips floated in a rectangular harbor. A sprawling marina and bar stood above. My heart jumped, and I paddled like mad. I didn't want to miss the inlet. I craved sugar. Peanut butter wasn't cutting it anymore. I sloshed into the bay past a tent pitched on the jetty. A canoe sat in the water just below it.

I beached my boat and walked up to the bar. The neon beer signs glowed and flashed in a bank of windows. The doors leading out toward the bay were wide open. Inside, the vinegary fug of spoiled beer clogged the air. It was a hot day but the air-conditioning was off, making the still, humid air unbreathable. After coming in out of the sun, I couldn't see anything and felt self-conscious standing in the doorway. My eyes adjusted, and I saw a couple of people wiping tables and turning chairs up on them. A man pushed a broom across the dance floor. He was sullen, with bags under his eyes. The bartender was stooped and tired. His eyes were bloodshot. I walked over to the bar and felt his hangover.

"Got a candy bar I can buy or a candy machine?" I said.

"No candy bars here, pal," the bartender said. He lit a cigarette. "Have a Coke on the house." He handed me a cold glass. The pop tasted like cigars.

"You're open?"

"Sure," he said. "We're always open after eleven. We just had a big party last night, band and everything. Musta been a hundert boats out there. It was like a riot."

A man sat at the bar, writing in a notebook. He was deeply tanned and wore thick horn-rimmed glasses. "You floatin' the river?" he said.

"Yes, I am."

"So am I," he said.

"I wonder if you're the guy they were talking about upstream?"

"What'd ya hear?" he said.

"A Jet Skier at Decatur told me a canoer had skipped the big lakes and was headed for Saint Louis."

"That's me," he said. "John Biondo."

John had a strong hand and burly forearms. He seemed very sad or depressed. I downed a few cigar-tasting pops because they were cold and sweet. I asked John if he could show me his rig, and we stepped out into the heat and walked down the jetty to his tent. I was glad to be out of the darkness and into moving air, even if it was a hundred degrees. The breeze off the river was furnace hot but was still better than the smell of stale beer and cigarette butts.

"I heard you had a rough time," I said.

"Miserable," he said, looking out over the river. "I got on the Missouri at Three Forks. A buddy of mine on his way to northern Montana dropped me off there. I had it good going to Great Falls. But I expected something more exciting, you know, something like the Yellowstone, whitewater and all that. But it was calm. Boring. Then I get to those big lakes, and the wind liked to push me back upstream."

He sat on a five-gallon bucket next to his tent and invited me to another.

"Past Helena," he said, "things were fine. But the river was high, and nothing was going on. I was waiting for the river to turn into something, you know."

"Well, for me, it was scary," I said.

"Nah," he said. "It wasn't nothin'."

"Didn't it do anything for you?"

"Sure, it was pretty and all," he said. "I was out West, you know, but I got a thing for Indian artifacts. I thought arrowheads and other stuff'd be everywhere on gravel bars. But the river was so high I never got to look around on gravel bars, cause there were no gravel bars."

A fish flopped in the water next to us. We sat in the full sun, and both of us sprouted sweat. John took off his shirt and swatted flies with it.

"I got Montana Power to drop me off at Morony Rapids just past that last dam there in Great Falls," he said. "It was night, but I said fuck it and paddled my ass off, just listening for the falls and rapids."

"You're kidding?" I said. I was in awe of him. "I heard stories about people getting killed there. I found a couple of people with the canoe club there in Great Falls. I'm glad I found them. They took me around the falls to Fort Benton."

"Those rapids at Morony were exciting for me," he said. "I made it through the Upper Missouri Wild and Scenic. It was scenic but not very wild. I mean no white water or anything."

"It was just the kind of river I hoped it would be," I said. "I never canoed before I started this thing."

"You're shittin'," he said.

"I knew dick about paddling a boat," I said.

"I bet you know now," he laughed.

"After I got through the Wild and Scenic River," he continued, "I saw that Fort Peck Lake on the map and said screw it. I called my buddy, who's on his way back to Saint Louis, and had him drop me off at Gavins Point."

"I did the same thing," I said. "I met a guy on Fort Peck Lake, only about thirty-some miles in, and he took me around to Wolf Point. I canoed the river to Williston and then, by some miracle, met another guy who took me around to Yankton."

"How do you feel about that?" he said. "I feel like I failed, you know. That I didn't do the whole thing."

"I don't feel so rotten," I said. "Well, I did, at first. I wish I'd canoed the lakes. But I think about my rig, how light it is, and how heartbreaking and frustrating that first bit in Fort Peck was. I didn't know what I was in for. I regretted it at first but not now. Not at all."

He turned serious and spoke only quietly. I thought he was going to cry. Behind those thick glasses his eyes were sad and filled with disappointment.

"Since Yankton it's just been hot," he said. "I'm homesick. The river's flooded. I got this girl who left me just before I started this trip on my mind.

"I feel so fucked. Even last night, there were a million people here. I just couldn't have a good time and went back out to my tent before the whole thing really ever started. I was in there just now trying to figure how I could get the boat to Saint Louis without having to go by river."

"Want to canoe together for a while?" I said.

"I'd like to, bud, but I'm hanging it up."

I really wanted a companion at this point. Being alone was fine. I liked it. But canoeing with someone would be better, even if we were only together a few days. I was going to talk him into going with me. I'd beg.

"Just give it a day or so," I said. "It'll be easier with someone else.

Let's say we don't get along after a few days or you don't get past this tough thinking—there're towns downstream where you could get your boat out just as easy. If we get to Kansas City together, I'll put you up until you get a ride. Or once I find my feet, I'll take you."

He thought about it while I went into the bar for another cola.

"Yeah, sure," he said, when I returned. "I'll canoe with you. I got nothin' to lose, and it might make me feel I didn't just give up."

We packed his gear and loaded his canoe, a sturdy, hefty boat made of plastic composite. A vinyl cover kept water out of the boat. A boot sewn into the cover cinched up around his body. Under the cover, in seven or eight five-gallon buckets, he had packed pounds and pounds of jerky, dried fruit, coffee, sugar, and flour. He had canned goods, crackers, pasta, and his camping gear and clothes. It was enough to feed and house one man for several months. He also had a .22-caliber plinking rifle, an ax, a garden spade, a heavy revolver, and water jugs. At about seven hundred pounds, his canoe with him and his gear weighed at least two and half times as much as my get up. He called his boat the "river barge."

We set off, and soon the river flowed between Omaha and Council Bluffs, Iowa. There was no bank. Brush, trees, and a floodwall prevented us from seeing anything of the cities. Traffic hummed, screeched, and banged around us, the sounds muted and distant. Rusting dolphins marked riverfront facilities, which, except for a dredger and a concrete plant, were long abandoned. Though we were in the middle of the cities, we could have been a thousand miles from them. No one would notice a thing we did. We were alone.

We set camp at a county park on the riverfront at Council Bluffs. It was a quiet place where a few families grilled dinners and listened to radios. We gathered wood and built a fire. John seemed to relax—tension and nervousness drained from him. The sun set, and long shadows folded together into night. Though the sky was clear, only a few points of stars broke through. Council Bluffs glowed on the hills in the distance.

"You know, it ain't so bad being on the river alone," John said. The campfire sent sparks into the still night. "But being lonely, that's bad. I was all right on this trip when I was alone. But the thought of this woman leaving me made me lonely. I love her, even though she hurt me. I want her back, you know, have our relationship again. But I just don't know how."

"Are you sure it's a good idea?" I said. "I mean it sounds like she made you crazy anyway."

"It was painful when she did it," he said. "Left me, I mean. But now's just worse. I can't stop thinking about her and being hurt."

"Think being alone with those thoughts getting tangled up makes it worse?" I said.

"That and a flood, and the wind, and the fucking mosquitoes."

"Let's stick together a few days and see what happens," I said. "We'll meet some folks, maybe shoot the guns, build big fires. It'll be different soon."

John did "tree work" in St. Louis and the surrounding area—slinging rope and trimming, pruning, and cutting down trees with a chainsaw. He learned the trade on his own and had never worked for anyone else. He lived humbly, earning enough money year to year to take long trips in an eighteen-foot Winnebago RV that also served as his house from time to time. Having grown up on the banks of the Missouri at its confluence with the Mississippi, he was fascinated with the river. But a long trip, alone, did not turn out the way he had hoped.

The next morning, I called my daughter and listened to her happy voice. She told me about the cartoons she was watching. I listened. Selfishly, I just hoped that she wouldn't feel I had abandoned her. I wanted her love and admiration more than anything in the world.

Later, I rested on the floor of my canoe and waited for John to finish packing his boat and cinch his cover down. I listened to the city. It filled the river with sound, day and night. Until I came into Yankton, the air had been filled with the sounds of animals, wind, trees, brush, water, rain, thunder, and tornadoes. The wind in a cottonwood had become the most beautiful sound I ever knew. There was something starkly lonely about the sound of a locomotive rumbling across the plain, the whine of tires on pavement in the distance, the bark of a dog echoing against the hills.

I wasn't bothered by the sounds of the city. They indicated activity, life, and society. I liked looking in from the outside, being the man no one noticed in the river. Hearing the sounds of the urban world, I found

I lusted for more of the human, industrial, urban, and suburban noise I would again become accustomed to and no longer notice.

The absence of human sound had driven John crazy. Since he had nothing to distract him from his pain, he bought a personal CD player in Helena. He had listened to it continuously, except when he ran out of battery.

As I was lying in my canoe, he walked up and offered me his CD player. He clipped in a Van Morrison record. I hadn't listened to music in over four months and hadn't missed it. On the river by myself, I sang and hummed to myself. I knew a few songs and made up more.

I put on the headphones, pushed play, and closed my eyes. Music and the human voice had never sounded so beautiful before. It overwhelmed me, and I began to cry. Tears fell down my temples. Noise, music, and talk were a part of my life at home. I wondered how I'd forgotten about how important they were. Suddenly, music seemed as much a part of me as the great silence I'd come to enjoy on the Upper Missouri.

The day was cloudy and windy and cool and dark. We canoed to the mouth of the Platte River, about fifteen miles, in just a few hours. I thought of the road I had walked next to the Platte through Nebraska and into Wyoming. How long ago that all seemed. I watched the Platte as we passed it. I thought of it starting as snowmelt in the Rockies, rushing down the North and South Platte Rivers to the plains where those two rivers met. The Platte joined the Missouri, and the Missouri sought the sea.

Up in Montana the Missouri had been a young and feisty river. Through the reservoirs, it grew in ways that I hadn't seen. But witnessing the water as it came through Gavin's Point Dam had shown me that it was still a strong river. The Platte helped the Missouri grow a little more on its way to the Gulf. And growth meant pain. Brusque undercurrents rocked our boats. John's boat, which rode deeper in the water than mine, listed from side to side in the swirling water.

"This one's a sumbitch," he said. He howled. Here voices didn't echo but rolled over the banks and onto the plains.

He loved the rough water. He stroked with kayak paddles in rhythm with the rocking of his boat, yelling as the boat jerked back and forth.

He raced far ahead, his boat and he becoming a speck in the distance. The sky soon broke up, and the Missouri reflected the blue and white of the puffy leftovers from the storm that never hit us. Among the clouds, John and his boat looked like an insect with tiny wings.

The next day wore into afternoon, and we decided to drift. We tied our boats together with rope and laid back and read books. The sun beat down on us; the day had grown hot. John never wore a life vest. I had worn mine every minute I'd been on the river since I'd started at Helena. I took it off now and felt lighter, fantastic. The current kicked us out toward the banks. We took turns paddling the boats back on course.

"You think there's much on the bottom of the river?" he said.

"Before the corps got a hold of it, I think the river was filled with plenty of stuff," I said. "I don't think there's much down there now but sand. I used to daydream about riverboat wrecks and treasure and that. But now that I've been on the river and seen it work, I don't think much stays in the channel. In the lee water, behind the wing dikes and jetties, there's probably a good collection of stuff."

"That's where they always find the bodies," he said. "Behind the dikes."

"I'd shit if we found a body," I said.

"Come on," he said. "It wouldn't be so bad. We'd land and go call somebody."

"I know," I said. "But the smell. Can you imagine what a body smells like on a day like this?"

"Like all of creation."

"That's too damn much humanity for me," I said.

John sat up from his book and reached under the canoe cover. As if the talk of death reminded him of his guns, he pulled out his .44 revolver. He checked the cylinder and snapped it shut.

"Why did you bring that along?" I asked.

"For protection," he said. "I went to school with a guy by the name of Eddy Harris . . ."

"The writer?"

"Yeah. You know his stuff?" he said.

"*Native Stranger* was one of the best travel books I ever read." Eddy

Harris was one of my favorite travel writers. I was happy someone else knew of his work.

"Well, you know in his first book, *Mississippi Solo*," John said, "how he shot at those racist fuckers who're givin' him trouble?"

"The guys in Arkansas," I said. "Yeah, I remember. That was scary for him, a black man in Confederate flag–waving redneck country."

"Well, when I planned this thing," he said, studying the pistol, "I was going to bring the rifle, just in case and to sorta break up the day. I thought maybe I'd get a rabbit or something to eat in case I lost the boat. Then I thought of Eddy needing a gun. And I know some of the people who hang out on the river, and they're not the coolest when it comes to strangers. So I brought the pistol."

"That's heavy freight," I said. "I'm not a gun guy. It changes the way you act around people, and I wanted to meet people."

"Yeah, but you never know . . . Crazy people."

"I met a few on the road to Helena," I said, "but only felt threatened three times. Weird stuff. Some guy in a car with his wife and kids. Another time before that, I felt a kind of malevolence when a guy slowed down on the highway near Lexington, Nebraska. I think he was looking me over to see if I was a woman. He pulled up, saw around the pack that I wasn't, and sped off."

"What about the third time?" he said.

"A woman in Lander, Wyoming, had offered to put me up for the night," I said. "The kids went to bed, and she put the moves on me. Ugly stuff. I guess she thought she was sexy, hiking up her shorts and pulling down her shirt. Her husband was in the next room."

"Maybe he was in on it," he said.

"I didn't know if it was that or if she was jacking with me," I said. "I'd a bolted, but if I ran or did something she didn't like . . . She starts screaming 'rape.' Her husband has a fat fucking gun. I wasn't going to get involved with it. And a gun would not have helped. What about you?"

"Nothing so far," he said. "But, you know, Montana and all those paranoid gov'ment haters. Bears on the Upper Missouri. That kind of thing. I'm glad I had it."

The river was now so straight in places it was as if we floated on a long, narrow lake. Both of us had been lonely. We had wanted to go home. Now that the ends of our journeys drew closer, we knew we could never go home. Home would look the same, but we would be different.

So when John raised the pistol level with the river, which flowed straight for a mile and a half into the next bend, I felt something good and powerful inside. I couldn't wait to get my hands on that .44.

The wallop of the shot shook the water into a thousand pearly pins around the front of his boat. We could see the bullet skip in a series of long splashes to the bend.

"Goddamn, John," I said. "There's a family eating at the dining room table down there and a bullet just bust the gravy boat."

"It won't come to nothin'."

He handed the pistol to me. The bank was littered in places with refuse that had drifted down from Omaha and Council Bluffs. There was not a lot of it but enough to find things to shoot at. My first bullet punched a hole in a plastic five-gallon bucket on the bank. I raised the pistol again and split a piece of limestone next to the bucket in half. A puff of chalk hung in the air.

Inspired, we defiled the grand Missouri and defiled it again: I shot like a Hollywood-movie hero, straight and true. I sunk an empty propane cylinder, a refrigerator, a gallon milk jug, and an old paint can. And John didn't do badly, either. A Styrofoam cooler lifted from the water and exploded into a thousand pieces of snowy fluff. He sank a tire on a rim with the shot after. He put holes in another five-gallon bucket with something in it we didn't want to know about and shattered a host of glass bottles. We busted cottonwood logs floating along with us into chunks and splinters. We took turns gunning down a bright-orange plastic kiddie car until it sank.

"Goddamn," he yelled. "Sinking plastic. There's nothing that gives a man more satisfaction than sinking plastic."

After a while, we settled back and smoked in the sun. I rigged John's fishing pole with a frog and lobbed it in the water.

"Now that fishing thing is downright dangerous," he said. "A guy could get mad and start shooting up the place. I haven't had a damn bit of luck with it, from Three Forks to here. Where are we now, Nowhere Special, Nebraska? That's something like two thousand miles of goddamn fishless void."

"I got some trout on the Upper Missouri before Great Falls," I said, "but haven't even tried since. It's too much trouble. Floating all day is good. Why fuss it up? In the evening, the last thing I wanna do is skin fish and run around looking for bait."

Elms and ash lined the banks. Groves of cottonwoods rose and fell as we drifted along. Forest-covered hills brought us into Nebraska City, where we pulled the canoes up to a wide boat ramp. The place was quiet except for wind in the cottonwoods. There were no people anywhere, but vans, cars, tents, and trailers stood at the campsites. One of the vans was similar to a friend's, Don Brown from Laramie, Wyoming. Closer, I saw the van indeed had Wyoming plates, and mail sitting on the front seat was addressed to Don. The good fortune of meeting with an old friend was almost too much to bear.

John and I set camp next to the bank and went to fill our water containers. The water, John pronounced, tasted terrible.

"Chlorine, my god," he said. "This is worse than some of that iron water upstream."

Water from wells and tiny municipal systems drawn directly from the ground had turned the inside of our collapsible water bags red. It had tasted sometimes like nails; other times, like garden dirt. But there was never any chlorine. In Yankton with the Christensens, I had been on a straight diet of iced tea, and so I had not tasted big-city water for some time. I passed the water under my nose. Sure enough—mustard gas.

"Can you believe we drink this stuff all the time at home?" he said. "It's bad; I don't know how I'll get used to it."

A few days on the river had cultivated a funk on us, comfortable and familiar, not noticeable until we felt we needed a shower. At the showers, we took turns standing in a hot version of that crappy water, and neither of us complained.

I was anxious to see Don. I'd met him at an AA meeting during my darker days in the History Department at the University of Wyoming. Slender and wiry, Don was about fifty, with red hair and a leathered face.

He always wore canvas hats with porcupine quills stuck into the brim. One night, I asked him about them. We were standing at the counter of a small diner in downtown Laramie. Don was drinking coffee.

"You know those big black things that look like trash bags in the road?" he said, lighting one of the thin, brown cigarettes he smoked. For a break from grading papers and doing thesis research I often took long drives outside of town at night. I'd noticed big black piles in and alongside the road that looked like trash bags. Not many, but enough.

"Yeah, I've seen them," I said. "They're porcupines?"

"That's right," he said. "Road-killed. You don't think Laramieites dump that much trash on the road, do ya?"

We laughed.

"The animal itself isn't so big," he said, "about the size of a small dog. They look so big because of the spines. I stop every now and then to pluck a few of them. I keep them in a drawer to use for various things, cleaning small holes in the van engine or tiny things around the house. They interest me. Hard, like metal, but hollow. They're sharp. The barbs stick into whatever decides to bother a porcupine and can't be pulled out the way they went in. You see, they have to travel all the way, say, through your hand if you tangle with one of them. You can't just pull them out once they're in. God's work, I say."

We had talked for a long time. Don sensed that grad school and I didn't go together well. Fussy, sensitive academics put me on edge. Around them, I felt my working-class upbringing, lack of refinement, and immaturity. I always either had a chip on my shoulder or felt inferior and insecure. I possessed no talent at navigating the fine points of academe. The tedium of academic endeavor and university paperwork unnerved me. My studies and anxiety over them kept me up at night. I was frazzled and fragile. Don could see it and turned the conversation to our mutual interest in nature and the outdoors: fly-fishing, hiking, and cross-country skiing.

"Say, why don't you come around?" he said. "I own a place in West Laramie, the Blue Sky Trailer Court. It's just six trailers. But I have some things out there that would interest you. We could also talk about getting you up to my cabin. It sounds like you could use a little time away."

"But I go backpacking almost every weekend up in the mountains somewhere," I said.

"Yeah, but the cabin'll be a nice switch."

For a weekend at the cabin, I drove west of Laramie to the Snowy Range through the tiny, fading settlement of Albany, once a stop on the defunct Wyoming and Colorado Railroad. The pavement ended at a Forest Service road that wound up into the heart of the Snowy Range. Don's cabin was just twelve feet square. It sat on a hill above Lake Creek, a small but fertile trout stream. He'd framed the cabin with lodgepole pine and walled it with plywood. It had one electric light and a hot plate. The woodstove warmed the one room and small loft quickly. Much more pleasant than the bare bulb was light from the oil lamps that stood around the cabin. There was a phonograph player in the loft and a stack of Ventures, Elvis Presley, and Johnny Cash records.

For the next year of school, and many times after, I spent days fishing the small creek, wandering the hills looking for signs of the secretive black bears of those parts, and sitting on the porch watching the pines grow. Evenings, I wrote in the glow of an oil lamp with Johnny Cash on the record player and fire crackling in the stove. Outside, the sneer of mountain lions echoed through the hills and over the sun-bleached log cabins of long-gone prospectors. Coyotes roamed the narrow valley around Lake Creek and yelped me to sleep.

Don and I became fast friends as he ushered me through the vagaries of sober life. More than one night during my time in Laramie, I slept on the narrow floor before the stove in his trailer at the Blue Sky Trailer Court, bathed in light from a mercury lamp high on a pole outside. After I returned to Kansas City, Don visited from time to time. He always slept in his van, where he had built a bed and had a cooler and a hot plate. My daughter loved him and still remembers him fondly today.

I was happy when Don drove into the Nebraska City riverfront park on his motorcycle a few hours after John and I set camp. Don explained he had been driving a cement truck on a highway project. He and John got along like gangbusters, telling stories and getting to know one another. Don had planned to go to an AA meeting that night and wanted me to go.

"But I have to make it an early one," he said. "The job starts at 5:00 a.m. about fifteen miles west of here."

Don and I rode into Nebraska City on the motorcycle he had brought on a trailer behind the van. We wound through the hills, and the speed made me dizzy. After the meeting, we motored off along quiet rural roads that unfolded between fields of beans and corn. At a point on the bluff upstream from the town, we stopped and looked out into the valley. My legs buzzed from the machine. My ears waited for the next rumble.

A warm breeze brushed the oaks around us. Down in the valley, on the Iowa side of the river, lights came on in distant farmhouses, mercury lamps on telephone poles illuminated farmyards — pools of blue.

"I'm just surprised to see you here," I said.

"There's no accounting for it," he said. "It's one of those things we get to talk about for a long time. How's the trip?"

"Good. I've seen a lot, learned some more. I was getting a little crazy until I met up with John."

"He seems like a good sort," he said.

"He is," I said. "He was having a bad trip. I think I'm helping him turn it around."

"People good?" he said, moving the discussion to my trip.

"Mostly. A coupla rough types, but no one who I didn't come away from with more than a dent in my ego."

"What about going home?" he said.

"I want to. I really want to be with Sydney."

"How's she these days?"

"Good, as far as I can tell," I said. "It's hard to get much over the phone. You know, mostly what's she's doing that moment."

"Not too tore up, I imagine."

"No," I said. "She asks me when I'm coming home. I tell her but she can't account for weeks or months."

"I wouldn't worry much," he said. "You're a better dad than you give yourself credit for."

"But I don't want to go home," I said.

"Life's too good on the river, eh?" He laughed.

"Exactly."

"It happens," he said. "Toughest part's to come. You're never gonna be the same, no matter what you try. So don't try. This is your new beginning."

We drove down a steep road and back through the town, now quiet and dark but for streetlamps. In downtown a traffic light above the Main Street kept order for no one in particular.

John had built a fire while we were gone and was watching it like people watch television. After Don went to bed, John and I walked up into town from the waterfront for something to eat. Both of us craved a hamburger and fries. In a small, dark bar, we asked the man behind the counter if he served burgers.

"I'm closin' for the night," he said. John and I looked at each other. It was only 9:30. "I can let you have a drink. But then you'll have to go up to the Hardee's."

"We're on foot," I said. "Is it far?"

"Just about five minutes that way," he said, pointing.

"Screw this," John said after about a mile. "That fuckin' guy didn't know what the hell he's talkin' about."

"That guy always drives," I said. "To him, it's just five minutes driving. For us, it's an hour."

We turned back through residential streets and woke up dogs. In downtown we found a bar on the Main Street that served food. A band of middle-aged men played Elvis and Bobby Darin covers. Loudly and badly. The place was crowded with people in jeans and sleeveless T-shirts, their hair shorn in front, long in back. The bartender slid a couple of frozen, precooked discs in a microwave and dropped a basket of limp potato slices into a deep fryer.

"It's a burger, anyway," John said.

Back at the park, we stoked up the fire again; listened to the tree frogs; and, after the last of the wood was burned, called it a good night.

17 Home but not Home

JOHN AND I CAME CLOSE TO LEADING PERFECT, HAPPY LIVES.
The next two weeks into Kansas City, we acted like a couple of Huck
Finns. We didn't try to stay away from people. Except for a few anglers,
there was no one to meet. Riverfront parks from Nebraska City on
were mostly abandoned. That was fine with us. Sandbars and woody
banks were better camping, anyway. We didn't care to see anyone. Our
company was enough.

Although we were always a step away from a road, a town, some
factory or farm, we could have been a thousand miles away from everywhere. The Missouri kept us isolated from the earthly influences of life
beyond the banks. In its immensity we were small and easy to overlook.
We wouldn't have known if anyone saw us anyway. I don't know about
John, but I didn't want to be found.

River life was simple and good. Each day, we boiled coffee and canoed
hard for a while. When the sun got past morning, we drifted until we
became bored or a nap ended, and then we paddled hard again until it
was time—that ill-defined "feels-like time"—to stop. To slow things
down, we stayed on sandbars for two nights running, because it pleased
us. The sky was always clear; the weather, hot and sticky. Evenings,
we abused fire because we had tons and tons of drift to burn. We ate
like kings and stayed up late watching the sky. We shot the rifle and the
pistol. We fished and caught nothing. We swam every day. We didn't
put on our shoes for two weeks, not once.

We camped one night at the Nebraska-Kansas border across the
river from the Iowa Indian Reservation. There, we witnessed one of
the most colorful and stunning sunsets either of us had ever seen. At
St. Joseph two days later, thick clouds of mosquitoes chased us into

our tents, and we missed the sunset. Instead, we cursed and mushed mosquitoes into the tent canvas. For the first time and only time, we did not build a fire.

Except for the mosquitoes, we had nothing of substance to complain about. Beavers, irritated by our invasions, slapped their tails on the water whole nights through. Combines harvesting the corn of early fall worked around the clock and kept us awake. But most of the time, the sound of machines and trucks and cars filled the days. In late evening, they abated, and it was then that we heard the frogs sing.

John felt better the closer we came to Kansas City. His mood lightened, and life became less serious to him. He wasn't over his girlfriend, but he was absorbing the fact that if someone doesn't want you around, well, you can't make them. He didn't know what his life would be like when he returned, but he was certain he'd take to the trees again. He knew he would always remain close to the river.

The leather thong that held the small pouch around my neck broke as we rounded the last bend into downtown Kansas City. The medicine bag Gordon Longtree had given me fell into my lap. The stones were still there, but the nature of the prayers had changed. Those prayers had become a part of me.

My journey through the Great Plains ended at the confluence of the Missouri and Kansas Rivers, the place where Kansas City was born. From the peninsula separating the two rivers, the river turned and headed east through the city. John had decided to canoe to St. Louis. He wasn't willing to give up life on the Missouri, not yet. As he paddled away, he thanked me for getting him this far and helping his river trip turn from "complete failure to absolute success!" His voice boomed off the flood wall. The river was glass smooth, and he soon became a speck on downtown Kansas City's skyline.

I called a friend from a nearby business and asked him to come pick me up. While I waited, I sat down on the bank. I looked up through the bridges and along the industrial waterfront. Beyond was a floodwall and the city behind it. Somewhere up there was my daughter. I rolled the medicine bag around in my pocket. I couldn't change the course of the river flowing though my life, I thought, and I didn't want to.

Epilogue

THE WOMAN I'D MET AT WOLF CREEK WAS RIGHT, AND SHE
was wrong. The Missouri consumed me, but didn't kill me. It saved me.
I began the trip intending for life to be different after I returned. I knew
before I arrived in Kansas City that the river had given me what I wanted
and more. The Missouri showed me I was more than a job, career, or
hobby or a member of any group. It made me do a whole growing up in
those two and half months. My friend Don Brown told me the toughest
part was to come but that I'd get on just fine if I tended to just what was
in front of me, not to the past or future.

Three and a half thousand miles of hand wringing about damaging my
daughter was fruitless. I didn't need confidence, the thing that I thought
would make my world right. I didn't need money. I didn't hit the river
bank magically endowed with fathering skills. All that mattered less than
finding out I'm persistent and willing to figure things out as they come.

With that much, then, Sydney and I built a good life together. She
entered kindergarten the school year following my summer on the river.
We often went camping, and I have taken her out on the river many
times. All through grade school and high school, I went to her sporting
events. I was and am her biggest fan.

I'd be a liar if I told you it was all sweetness and light. I was often
frightened and unsure. I wasn't always patient, and I regret that the
most. Sydney lived in two houses with very different people, each of
whom had their own ways of looking at life. That's not easy for a kid.
As a young adult and now out on her own, she's had her problems. But
fortunately, she visits, calls me on the phone, and trusts me. I can think
of no greater return for a father's love.

When Sydney was eight, I fell in love with and married Virginia

Lesco. Our life together has given me a kind of security I never knew before. Ten years later, we adopted our son, Nicholas. He was four and half when he joined us. Shortly after his arrival, I thanked Syd for teaching me how to be a father. Because of that, it was easier to be Nick's father. I was sorry, I said, for not knowing what I was doing, for being impatient, for being scared and often harsh.

"That's all right, Dad," she said. "I didn't know how to be a kid, either."

If you remember, I spoke about a local paper that published my notes from the road. They were small columns, biweekly accounts of life on the plains and the river. Insignificant as they were, those reports started my ten-year journalism career. When I returned from Montana, I freelanced stories for the newspaper and within a year joined the staff. There, I spent three years doing what I could to change my world. I exposed corruption, told stories of success and failure, and comforted the afflicted and afflicted the comfortable, as Mother Jones would say. It was the first job I'd ever had where I didn't start to rot after a few months. I became tired, and I fell into ruts but got back out of them. That job would have kept me for a long time, but the owner sold the newspaper three years after I started writing for it. The new regime didn't suit me, and I moved on. I freelanced stories for other publications for a long time after.

It turns out that long journeys don't change a person completely. I went to work for a book publisher and fell back into the old traps. I was good at what I did and made a ton of money — not riches, mind you, but a good living. After just a short time, I found myself sitting at a desk wondering why I hadn't found fulfillment. I came into the office late and left early. I took two-hour lunches. After three years, two and a half years longer than I should have stayed, I quit and felt good about it.

I spent a year making even more money than ever, doing whatever work I came across. I built rock walls, painted houses, and hauled refuse in my pickup. Then I entered a doctoral program in history at the University of Missouri–Kansas City and later became an ironworker. I found balance teaching history and Western civilization at a fine community college not far from here. I teach during the school year and build bridges in the summer. I can think of no finer fate.

The Missouri's the only river I've ever canoed. I still spend time with it. Weekends. Weeks. John Biondo and I remain close friends today. I have visited him many times. When I canoed to St. Louis on the Missouri in 2005, John met my good friend Gary Jenkins and me at the boat landing at the Columbia Bottoms Conservation Area. He took me back to Kansas City. Since then, we talk about once a month. We agree that people build the strongest bonds between each other when they share work, food, fishing, or a trip on the river.

While we don't often talk about our trip on the river anymore — we are well beyond that now — we still often wonder aloud what it would feel like to have a pocket full of cash and be unhappy. Or happy and rich. Whatever.

I didn't realize it when I landed at the confluence of the Missouri and Kansas Rivers in 1995, but I'd been looking into the river and seeing myself not as a completed person but as a process. I'm not a good student and, often, not a good historian. I'm not the cleverest, fastest, or most skilled father, husband, ironworker, writer, teacher, or historian. But I'm trying.

I can thank the Missouri for showing me the persistent, indefatigable side of myself, that part of me that carries me through fear, insecurity, and want.

I often watch the river from a hill near downtown Kansas City where the Corps of Discovery camped. I live in the neighborhood and walk only one minute to a point where I can see the river. Perhaps the contemplative moment I have when I stand before it gives me new insights into myself. Dams, levees, and limestone riprap banks can't constrain the river forever. A job, routine, and social expectations only hold me as long as I want them to. Then I will walk away from them. I know now that I carry afflictions of my own making and lay them down when I am tired. Figuring that out, I think, has been my salvation.

But I think salvation is not static. You can't get it and keep it. It comes and goes. I've found that my redemption is the hardest work I face every day. And that's when I find comfort in the river. It changes in its seasons and at our hands. But it endures. The Missouri River will always be there when I want to come home. I find faith in that.